Foreword by Jack R. Taylor

Learning to Give Thanks FOR All Things

Rick Carr

What People Are Saying About This Book

"While reading Extreme Gratitude, I was deeply touched by the phrase author Rick Carr wrote in defining gratitude as 'the language of the Kingdom.' As I read further, I was constantly reminded that everything we see and everything we are is for and about the Kingdom of God. How does one find the Kingdom of God or the grace to be grateful when faced with a diagnosis of cancer or the loss of a loved one, or when faced with any myriad of life-crushing circumstances? We have but to remember the language of the Kingdom and walk in extreme gratitude. We will all walk through moments of extreme heartache in this life, but the overlying truth found in this book puts it all in perspective. Extreme circumstances call for extreme hope. Extreme hope is found in our relationship with the Extreme God, Who is Lord of All. Extreme moments of fear require faith in our God's extreme love for us. Knowing the language of the Kingdom of God launches us into the deeper places of an intimate relationship with our Extreme God. Do you desire deeper intimacy with our God? Do you desire to know how to find hope when faced with the loss of absolutely everything you hold dear? Practice extreme gratitude. I highly recommend Extreme Gratitude to any who dare desire an ever-deepening intimacy with the God Who loves us extremely."

Dennis Jernigan
Husband, Father of Nine, Grandfather of Eleven,
Song Receiver, Author, Worshiper

"A wise man said, 'We are not human beings having a spiritual experience; we are spiritual beings having a human experience." 'As a spiritual being giving thanks is the most natural, logical thing we can do.

As a human being giving thanks can be the most difficult thing, we do. Giving thanks to God in every experience in life is one of the most important indicators of spiritual maturity. This book will give reasons for giving thanks, examples of giving thanks, and results for giving thanks.

Rick Carr lets us walk with him in the pages of this book as he learns to walk in the spirit, experiencing God's way of thinking. One of the powerful illustrations you will read is how at a shopping mall, he had to walk off justifiable anger. While walking, he chose to thank God instead of being angry over unfair treatment. As soon as he gave thanks to God, the unfair treatment swiftly changed to favorable treatment. Giving thanks to God changed him. God changed the circumstances for him. You will read many real-life experiences and find a sure scriptural foundation for being a thankful person. As you finish the book and read his conclusion, you will find yourself better equipped to give thanks in all things. You will be thankful that you can give thanks."

Jim Hylton
Staff Pastor
Northwood Church,
Keller, Texas

"I was very moved by *Extreme Gratitude*. It demonstrates an understanding of scripture, life experiences, faith and perseverance in the face of uncertainty, and reveals the true attributes and journey of being a follower of Christ. Rick is a true scholar, and an example of what it means to be a Christian."

Tyson Cobb
Director, Pastor, and Evangelist,
Go Follow Jesus International

"*Extreme Gratitude* is a book written for an hour such as this!

Rick has done an amazing job including his personal testimony and journey with the Lord in bringing to life the scriptures that give us reason to be extremely grateful in all things!

This book left me feeling even more confident in the greatness and goodness of the One who is working all things at this moment in time according to the council of His will. After reading this I'm absolutely convinced that the way we get in is the way we go on, and what God began in us He will complete regardless of what life throws at us."

Dr. David White
Senior Pastor of the Gathering Church
Moravian Falls, NC

"I first met Rick at a Spiritual Son's Gathering for our mutual spiritual father, Jack Taylor. I was immediately gripped with Rick's humility and the purity of his pursuit of the Kingdom. In Extreme Gratitude, Rick communicates the deep Kingdom truths of Scripture with ease while weaving in engaging stories and practical life application. My favorite part of this book was that it felt like a personal letter from the heart of the Father to me the reader. It caused me to give thanks and live with extreme gratitude for all the Lord has done. I believe you will experience the same."

Jay Moeller
Senior Pastor,
Legacy Church
New Braunfels, Texas

Copyright © 2020 Rick Carr
ISBN: 9798639057656
Library of Congress Control Number: 2020909856
Published in the United States of America

All rights reserved as permitted under the U. S. Copyright Act of 1976. No part of this publication may be reproduced, distributed, or transmitted in any form or by any means, or stored in a database or retrieval system, without the expressed written permission of the author and publisher.

Unless otherwise noted, scriptures are taken from the *New American Standard Bible*®,© Copyright 1960, 1962, 1963, 1968, 1971, 1972, 1973, 1975, 1977, 1995 by The Lockman Foundation. Used by permission." (www.Lockman.org).

Scripture quotations marked NCV are taken from the *New Century Version*®. Copyright © 2005 by Thomas Nelson, Inc. Used by permission. All rights reserved.

Dedication

To my loving and dearly loved wife. Trish, you have walked this journey with me. We have learned these lessons, and are still learning, together. I cannot imagine this journey without you. Thank you for your example of love for and faith in the Lord, and for constantly supporting and encouraging me in life and in my pursuit of things above.

To our children: I hope and pray that observing my process of learning, occasionally seasoned with stumblings and failings, has not obscured the truth. May you each continue to learn and grow— in faith, in rest, and in giving thanks to God.

In memory of Jean Ellzey: Aunt Jean had the greatest influence on my life of any single person I have known because her love and example was a key factor in setting me on this course. God was her best friend. She was born blind and crippled. She never walked without assistance or saw the light of the sun, but she consistently walked by faith in the Light of the Son. Now she is worshiping her Lord and Savior with a full strong voice, beholding His face, and "running around, seeing people."

In memory of Dr. L. Jack Gray, who heavily influenced my life, and thereby this work.

Acknowledgments

My brother, Pat, who helped proofread my manuscript. Thank you for your time and your insights. By the way, I love you.

Tim Taylor, you have blessed me as pastor, friend, and now publisher. Thanks for giving me a shot at this, and thank you for all your time and help getting it to print.

Our home church fellowship, Glenn and Anita, Adam and Julie, and Keri—thank you for sharing a season of 16 years together. Thank you for encouraging me to teach this material and to develop the study guide for it.

Steve G, Brian D, Dennis J, Joe G, and David R—dear friends through the years—for hours spent talking, sharing, worshiping, encouraging, challenging, questioning, and loving. Thank you, dear brothers.

Contents

Dedication
Acknowledgments
Foreword By Jack R. Taylor
Introduction   15

    Chapter 1   To Know Him   27
    Chapter 2   The Atoning Work of Christ   37
    Chapter 3   Corn Kernel Christianity   45
    Chapter 4   The Sabbath Rest   55
    Chapter 5   Dead Faith or Dead Works?   67
    Chapter 6   Extreme Righteousness   79
    Chapter 7   Little Faith   87
    Chapter 8   Our God Does Whatever He Pleases   99
    Chapter 9   God's Purpose   105
    Chapter 10 God's Purpose Continued   115
    Chapter 11 Extreme Thanks   119
    Chapter 12 Extreme Benefits   129

Conclusion   143

Addendum   147
Endnotes   155

About the Author

Foreword

This book speaks to the question:

"I Am Loved, So What?"

Extreme Gratitude is a book to which you will want to return again and again. It could be entitled "The Other Side of Grace." When the revelation that we are loved takes place, the natural thing is to feel and practice that love so graciously that we tap into grace which enables us to love as we are loved.

This volume will spur the response of extreme thanksgiving, which will likely produce extreme acceptance, which love will elicit from the one loved in a grace, which always is expressed in gratitude. Rick Carr, in an extremely healthy, healthy love experience, shows us love in action.

May God bless the reader with the kind of thankfulness that will exhibit the attitude of the extreme of God's love!

Jack Taylor,
President,
Dimensions Ministries,
Melbourne, Florida

Introduction

October 24, 1864, was a cool Fall day in south Louisiana. It was preceded by several days of brisk skirmishes with flying rifle balls and falling artillery shells. It preceded several days of cold, pelting rain. But this day, Coleman Sibley found time to sit for a few minutes and get a taste of home, writing a letter to his wife, Lizzie. He was a lieutenant in the Confederate army, serving in the ongoing Red River Campaign in south Louisiana. She was keeping the farm. When the war began, they had two little girls. Ella was 3, and Belle was born in March 1861. The oldest had died earlier in April 1864. Coleman wrote:

> "A mother's duty to her children is very great. The future life of your sweet child depends very much on your teaching and example before her. Be firm yet kind, never tired of doing for her. Let her know that you pray for her soul and that you wish her to be pious. Lizzie dear, have you ever learned her yet that there is a God who rules over her destiny. I fear this is a subject that you avoid. But dear, beware that you do so while she is yet young. Show her the rising sun, the bright moon, the growing plant, the stately tree, the fragrant flower, the falling rain, and such things, and teach her that they are made by a great and good God who loves her and who will save her in life and after death. Teach her to love the name of God and worship him while she is young, and she will not forget to do so when she is old. Learn her to love everything that is good and beautiful. Point her to heaven and tell her that she will meet her sister there again, where they will stay together always and be parted no more. Tell her God called little Ella home and does so to all others who die. Darling, I pray that you will not neglect your duty in this for in you rests a great responsibility—God will bless you if you ask His aid with the proper spirit."

Coleman returned home on furlough for a few weeks in mid-January 1865, and returned home to stay in June of that year. John Coleman Sibley, Jr., was born in November. As was the case with many returning soldiers, Coleman's health was compromised by his exposure to the elements during the war. John was five and Belle was nine when he died in 1870. Nancy tried to hold things together. She moved to New Orleans where she was able to find work. She died in 1874, leaving Belle, 13, and John, 9, orphaned. Lizzie's mother, Matilda, took them in and raised them on a farm a few miles up the road from where they were born. When Matilda passed away, John inherited the farm.

In the late 1920's, one of John's daughters, Ruth, moved with her family to live with John on his farm. Ruth and her husband had two little girls. One was my mother, Earline, and the other was my Aunt Jean. To them, John was Papa Sibley. He loved God and had a significant influence on both of the girls.

Jean was born blind, crippled, dwarfed, with brittle bone disease. She was bright, perhaps a little precocious, and unaware that she was blind, much less what that meant. She did know that she could not run and play like other children. Earline and their friends and cousins would sit and play with Jean. Before long, though, someone would want to play a more active game, and Jean would be left sitting alone.

Papa Sibley took note of this and would make a special effort to spend time with Jean himself. They would sit in the swing, or in his room, or go for walks. She wrote in her autobiography:

> "My grandfather, John Coleman Sibley, whom we lovingly called Papa, ... has had the greatest spiritual impact on my life of anyone I have ever known. He was a devoted Christian and was loved and respected by all who knew him ....
>
> "Living on the farm was fun. One of my happiest experiences was going for walks with Papa. Going for walks meant riding on his shoulder as he walked about

outside, describing flowers, trees, grass, and all the things that God created to make His world beautiful. I loved the sounds and smells of nature, and I loved flowers, especially roses ....

"I loved the animals, and Papa showed me how things grow. He showed me what it was like to pick cotton, and he permitted me to ride his horse. No matter what we were doing, he always reminded me that all that we have comes from God.

"I remember riding in a wagon to a little country church when we did not have a car. It was in God's plan for us to live on Papa's farm for a period of time. I received spiritual blessings and had opportunities that I would never have known if we had not lived there."[1]

Papa Sibley lived out in his relationship with Jean the very thing his father, Coleman, had encouraged Lizzie to do, in a letter written 60 years to the day before Jean was born.

It gets even better, though, from my perspective. Jean lived with her mother until Ruth died in 1958. My parents began looking for a larger house where the four of us could live and where Aunt Jean could come live with us. I was five, and my brother was nine when we moved into the new house.

I was told I shouldn't bother Aunt Jean, but like Jesus, she opened her arms to little children. I spent many hours over the years sitting with her in her room. She would tell me stories from the Bible, read to me from books that had Braille on one side and pictures and print on the facing page. She would read to me from her Braille Bible, and tell me stories of her childhood. She encouraged me to read the Bible and pray and shared the things God was teaching her. She followed the path laid out by my great-great-grandfather and passed on to her by my great-grandfather.

My parents also loved the Lord and were active in church. We attended church pretty much "whenever the doors were open." When I was seven and became aware there was sin in my life, I knew where to turn. On September 11, 1960, with the faith of a child, I entered the Kingdom of Heaven. At the age of nine, I believed God was calling me to the ministry.

I thought God wanted me to be a missionary. Shortly before leaving home for college, I had the opportunity to lead singing for revival services at Levy Street Mission in Shreveport. This little church was sponsored by the First Baptist Church of Shreveport. It was in a poor part of town that was a blend of industrial and residential—a rough part of town. Most of the congregation lived in rundown homes or apartments, or government housing projects. Even so, the joy and enthusiasm of the congregation as they sang blessed me. Their faces all but radiated with their love for and joy in the Lord. The next Sunday, in my home church, we were singing a hymn when I felt compelled to look around. The faces of the congregation looked so bored and disinterested. The thought came to my mind as though it were being spoken to me, not originating from me: "I don't need you in foreign missions; I have plenty for you to do in this country." I knew the Lord was speaking to my heart. This was in the 1970s, and since the prevailing ideology said God only called people to be preachers or missionaries, I went off to college to prepare for the pastorate.

Over the years and through a series of events, which I'll share in part later, I realized God had other plans for my life. By then, I'd graduated college with a major in Religion and minor in Greek, and had two years of seminary training behind me. Nonetheless, I entered the ranks of the laity. Like most Christians, I spent a good portion of Sunday morning in a pew with little or no opportunity to share what God was teaching me. The church had taught me all my life to study, to learn, to know God for myself. A core doctrine of the Baptist denomination was the "priesthood of the believer." Yet when your average everyday believer begins to truly learn and grow, there is little opportunity given for him or her to share what he or she is learning. They can teach a Sunday school class. There might be an opportunity to teach a Sunday evening class. However, there aren't many other opportunities given.

EXTREME Gratitude

When the pastor is absent, he usually calls in another preacher, maybe out of retirement, or a missionary on furlough or some other professional to "fill the pulpit." Rarely is someone from the congregation given the opportunity.

Silly me. I believed what I'd been taught. I believed that God cared about me, had a plan for my life, wanted me to know Him, wanted me to grow spiritually, wanted me to evangelize and to disciple others. I believed in the priesthood of the individual believer. I was free to go before Holy God on my behalf. I had the additional training of college and graduate studies that gave me the same tools for this as most of the pastors at the churches I attended.

It reached a point where my heart ached within for an opportunity to share. It was as though I were being filled to overflowing with what God was showing me, but there was no outlet. I identified with Ezekiel, who was sent to speak to the Israelites, but when he arrived, God didn't give him anything to say for several days—except *my* "days" were turning into years.

Writing gave me some release. It gave me a way to get out what was in me. If nothing else, it would be available for my wife and children. I didn't know if anyone else would ever see it, but at least they would have documentation of things I shared with them and a way to remember it after I was gone.

At the time, I was working for Word Records. Word had two separate divisions, one for music and one for books. I asked Kip Jordan, an editor and Vice President of Word Publishing, if he would be willing to read my manuscript and give me some feedback on the book itself and whether it would be worth attempting to get it published. I knew that since I wasn't famous or pastoring a large congregation, Word wouldn't publish it. I just wanted the feedback.

After reading it, he told me it should be published. He gave me some suggestions on the kind of company to look for as a first-time author. I was encouraged and looked through some lists of publishers.

By then, we were attending AnchorChurch in Fort Worth. It was founded by Tim and Jack Taylor. Tim's vision was for a church where believers met on Sunday morning for worship and preaching, and one night a week with a homegroup of about 4 to 6 families, and the rest of the week just lived the Christian life in simple, practical expression. The ministry of the church was to be done by the congregation through the cell groups. Many people referred to Jack as the pastor, because he was the guy in the pulpit pretty much every Sunday. Jack said upfront he was not the pastor. He was the preacher; we were the ministers. Jack preached on Sunday morning. He was a noted author, and during the week, he spoke at conferences and seminars around the country.

AnchorChurch and some subsequent church and ministry opportunities answered the cry of my heart to share the lessons God had quickened in me, at least on some level. Other than using it to teach, the book went on the shelf, and I didn't pursue getting it published.

I wrote the original manuscript for this book nearly 30 years ago, though I have updated it a couple of times since then. At the time I wrote it, I fully believed what I was writing. I knew it was truth, and I was living it as best I knew how. Over the years, I have experienced it more and more, learning to apply it in all areas of my life. When I wrote the original introduction and included the phrase, "Cancer? Me?" I never thought that phrase would apply to me.

In late 2008, I noticed a swelling in some lymph glands in my neck below the jawline. It had happened before in response to random sinus infections but always cleared up when the infection did. This time it lingered, then got larger. In May 2009, a severe, persistent sinus infection sent me to the doctor. He noticed the lump on my neck and referred me to an ear, nose, and throat specialist. A CT Scan led to a biopsy, which showed a malignancy. That was followed by a PET Scan to determine how widespread the cancer was, which would help determine a treatment regimen. It was determined it had probably started in my tonsils. Although it was at least stage three, having spread to the nearby lymph glands, it was a "very treatable" cancer, and the prognosis was good from the start, though not certain. Nonetheless, it got my attention.

As all this was unfolding, my first thoughts were, "It's time to put up or shut up. I have to stand on what I know is true. I have to live the things I believe and have spent my life sharing." I had written this book. It proclaimed principles I had taught in various classes, in discipleship relationships, in Bible study groups, in home church meetings, and in sermons through the years. I had lived it in what I had faced up till then. This was different. This was "the C-word."

Once you've been told you have cancer, you realize how fragile and uncertain life is. The doctors could find nothing in my lifestyle on which to blame cancer in my throat. There's no history of cancer in our family. I don't use any tobacco, drink, overeat, or do anything else consistently or in excess to stand as an apparent cause. The surgeon removed my tonsils and found and removed a cancerous spot in my throat. Three weeks of recovery from the tonsillectomy was followed by seven weeks of radiation, chemo, and then another surgery to remove the affected lymph nodes. So, my treatment lasted in all about five months. I lost my sense of taste for several months. Thanksgiving dinner sure looked good, but I couldn't taste it. When taste began to return, it took a few months for things to taste the way they did before. A few things still don't. My throat and neck are not as elastic as they were before radiation.

I'm over ten years out, and I'm cancer-free. I'm here to tell you I still believe what I've written in this book. The truths I share here with you have seen me through. I found peace in the storm. It was still a storm, and it wasn't always easy. I can say unequivocally, God is. God is faithful. God is worthy to be trusted to the point that you can give thanks in and for all things. I pray that as you read, you will find the foundation for believing for yourself that God truly is and that He truly is a rewarder of those who seek Him.

This book touches a number of principles of Christian living. The first few chapters may seem to have no relation to the stated subject of "extreme gratitude." I believe they are essential to establishing an understanding of the kind of faith to which we are a called, and out of which, true thankfulness, extreme thankfulness can and must flow. It is about learning to rest with a Sabbath rest kind of rest. When we learn to enter into the Sabbath Rest that remains to the people of God, it will affect our health, our family, our friendships, our devotional life, everything. It is about dying to self. It is about being crucified with Christ, bearing our cross, walking in newness of life. It's about entering into and living in His Kingdom. It's about becoming an overwhelming conqueror through Jesus Christ. It's about righteousness that exceeds religion. It's about seeing Satan and the world made of no effect in our lives, and the ability of God Himself turned loose in and through us. It's about a God who is worthy of our total trust and desires to reward those who seek Him with the greatest blessings.

Ultimately, it is about faith in God. Trusting God is both a doorway into rest and a result of learning to rest. I believe with all my heart it finds its sincerest expression in the language of the Kingdom—giving thanks. Gratitude is a feeling of thankfulness in response to grace. Thanks is an expression of that gratitude.

Thanksgiving is not just "an attitude of gratitude." Websters Dictionary defines attitude as, "a manner of acting, feeling, or thinking that shows one's disposition, opinion, mental set, etc.; one's disposition, opinion, mental set, etc." What we are talking about goes beyond disposition or opinion. Mindset might be appropriate in that Paul says, "set your mind on things above." The word he uses is present tense imperative. In other words, it's a command to keep on thinking about, keep the mind focused on, spiritual things.

EXTREME Gratitude

Many books and articles encourage us to be thankful. An "attitude of gratitude" isn't a bad thing. It is just ultimately insufficient. It's a great place to be, a great attitude to foster, to develop and maintain. However, in application, it can just be another version of a positive attitude. You find the good in a situation and say thank you. You don't necessarily need to have anyone to whom you are saying thank you. You can just "be thankful." Some of the popular writings have focused on looking for opportunities to say thank you to other people. It can "make their day." It can be a blessing that contagiously affects the attitudes of those to whom we direct our thanks. It can diffuse a tense moment, stop an open conflict, heal old wounds. All these things are beyond good.

The thankfulness to which we are encouraged in Scripture exceeds this, to the extreme. It is extreme in its object. We are expressing our thankfulness to the Creator of the entire universe, the cosmos, all that exists. It is extreme in its subject. We are encouraged to give thanks for all things, as in **all** things. It is extreme in the time we are to give to it. We are to give thanks **always** for all things. It is extreme in its source. It comes from a heavenly perspective on life, the world around us, our situation, and experiences; indeed, on all things. It comes from placing our faith in God and seeking Him, His righteousness, and His perspectives. As a result, it is extreme in its effect. It goes beyond feeling good, diffusing conflict, and healing old wounds. It puts us even more in tune with the mind of God, takes our faith to new levels, and impacts our lifestyle, our relationships, and our physical, emotional, and mental health. It is extreme in its process. As with all aspects of the Christian life, it is not something we master instantaneously. It is something we learn, embrace, grasp, think we know, and then realize we are still learning it years later. Growth is a process. It takes time. Giving thanks always for all things is something we learn to do over and over, as we face each new "thing" that is a part of the "all things" in life. You may have it mastered in everything you've faced up till now. Then, you hit a crisis like none you have ever experienced before. Or, you may realize that it applies to some crisis you did face before, but have not fully dealt with. In either case, reaching a point of giving thanks for even this most dreaded, hated, despicable condition or situation becomes an entirely new learning experience.

Christianity centers around an extreme God. This one God declares Himself the one and only, true and living God, yet He finds expression in the extreme form of three persons – Father, Son, and Holy Spirit. He spoke, and the extremely vast universe came into being and is still expanding through the cosmos on the wave of His initial command as our scientists and astronomists continue to discover "new" stars and galaxies. This magnificent creator of all things created man out of dust into which He breathed His breath. He instilled life, His image, a desire for fellowship, and the freedom to choose faith and love. He knew man would ultimately choose to place his faith in himself, so before creation, He put in play an extreme plan of reconciliation. At the proper time, this extremely large God wrapped Himself in that same limited, human flesh, taking it to the extreme of coming as an infant, in order to restore man to fellowship with God. Jesus called us to an extreme Kingdom, characterized by an extreme righteousness, which can only be experienced through extreme faith, which learns to be thankful at an extreme level that encompasses "all things."

These are principles of Christian living that help answer some of life's tough questions:

"God! WHY?"

"What am I supposed to learn through this?"

"I just don't understand why all this is happening to me!"

"Why did my wife leave the kids and me?"

"Why is my child living a life of sin?"

"Why does my husband drink?"

"Why did my dad make those visits to my room when I was little?"

"Cancer? Me? Why Lord?"

EXTREME Gratitude

"God, don't you care?"
"I THOUGHT YOU WERE A LOVING GOD?!"

God's Word seems to set forth some very clear guidelines to answer these questions. Maybe I'm being too simplistic about this. Then again, maybe being "simplistic" is just exercising the "faith of a child" to which He calls us. Maybe it is time the body of Christ "simply" accepted what God is doing. Or just maybe, we have failed to realize that God is doing something. I suspect that we do not believe that God is active. As we look at the world around us, we see only that which is obvious to our senses, and much of it is not good.

God created man to live in His Kingdom from day one. He placed man in a garden and, subject only to the higher authority of God Himself, gave man dominion over the earth. We have come to accept that we lost that dominion in the fall. We forfeited to Satan and believe he now is the prince of this world and the dominant force in world events. We agree with the writer of Hebrews, who quotes from Psalm 8:6, "Thou hast put all things in subjection under his feet." This verse is saying that God has subjected all things to man. The writer goes on, "For in subjecting all things to him, He left nothing that is not subject to him. But now we do not yet see all things subjected to him" (Heb. 2:8). Unfortunately, we stop there. We miss out on the glorious hope given us in verses 9-18.

As He does with each of His children, God has taught me many lessons from many passages of scripture through many experiences. Eventually, these lessons began to mesh together as part of a whole. They are not disassociated lessons, each with its own application in different areas of life, so much as they are part and parcel of the kingdom plan of God.

For too long, the church has separated spiritual truths about discipleship and growth from practical application and ministry. Even when they attempt to teach both, it seems many Christians talk about the teachings of Jesus regarding the cross and denying yourself and rest and place them in one box. Then they talk about ministry, witnessing, discipleship, and other aspects of Christian living as a completely separate line of teaching. Rarely are the two ever meshed. Rarely are the spiritual truths shown to be the foundation, the motivation, and the power for accomplishing the practical. As a result, we never get around to a clear, effective proclamation of "Jesus Christ, and Him crucified." It's as though we don't believe that message can truly affect the way people live, and so we have to add to it or avoid it altogether.

Again, the truths shared in this book are only truly learned over a period of time. Even when you think you know them, there is more to learn of them. It is a process. In talking about death to self, for example, I am often asked, "How do you do it?" Although I understand the process, and I am walking in it, it is difficult to share in brief, concise terms. So, in hopes of coming up with a good summary answer to this question, I put it to one of my mentors, Dr. Jack Gray. I was in my mid-30s, and he was 75 years old at the time and had been walking in these truths a lot longer than I had. His response was, "I am not sure I can come up with a succinct answer, because I do not have a completed experience."

I like that. It didn't give me the concise answer I was looking for, but it did sum up the process very nicely.

Chapter 1

To Know Him

> "*But whatever things were gain to me, those things I have counted as loss for the sake of Christ. More than that, I count all things to be loss in view of the surpassing value of knowing Christ Jesus my Lord, for whom I have suffered the loss of all things, and count them but rubbish so that I may gain Christ, and may be found in Him ... having a righteousness ... which is through faith in Christ, the righteousness which comes from God on the basis of faith, ... that I may attain to the resurrection of the dead."*
> Philippians 3:7-11

What things were gain to me? I was born and raised in a Christian family. I was always a "good kid." I was a leader in the youth group at church, and class chaplain through most of high school. I helped found a Christian service club at both of the high schools I attended. I was called into vocational Christian service at the age of nine, fully convinced I was to be a pastor or missionary. I attended a Baptist college, majoring in religion and minoring in Greek. I married a good Baptist girl who said she was called to be a pastor's wife. She played the piano and was church pianist at the churches I served as Music and Youth Director or Interim Pastor. We sang duets together in church. I was Chaplain's Assistant at Central Louisiana State Hospital, where I counseled patients and led singing and preached at worship services on the wards.

My good name was gain to me. The respect of my peers, parents, aunts, uncles was gain to me. Serving the Lord in "the ministry" was gain to me. Knowing what I was going to do with my life was gain to me. Having a wife who shared that ministry was gain to me. Going to seminary was gain to me.

I lost it all. The marriage was stormy, mainly we both were young, immature, quick to get hurt, or offended. In addition, she married me to get away from her alcoholic parents and "hoped the love part would come later." After a few years, she decided she wanted out, and left. (That's the short version - relationships are always more complicated than that, and we share responsibility for the failure of our marriage.) All those dreams, all those things I counted as gain, slipped through my fingers.

> *"My sheep hear My voice, and I know them, and they follow Me; and I give eternal life to them, and they will never perish; and no one will snatch them out of My hand. My Father, who has given them to Me, is greater than all; and no one is able to snatch them out of the Father's hand. I and the Father are one."*
>   John 10:27-30

Because He never let go of me, I realized that I had been clinging to all the trappings the world could offer a young man going into the ministry, more than I was clinging to Him. Because He never let go of me, I learned that all those things I had been clinging to were temporal. (Sorry folks, but your earthly ministry is not in itself eternal. It will burn. It may or may not have eternal *results*, but when this world comes to an end, it will burn.)

Whatever you are clinging to: a job, a ministry, "the" ministry, your father, or mother, husband or wife, or children, or brothers, or sisters, yes, and even your own life—let go. Fall into the Father's arms. Nothing can snatch you from there. Cling to Him. Seek Him first, and His righteousness and everything else you need in life will be added back to you. Quit trying to get your needs met. Meet *Him*. Love *Him*. Seek *Him*. Know *Him*. Count all those things you have considered to be gain or a benefit to yourself to possess, as loss.

Now go beyond that. Go beyond the things you count as gain. Count, (are you ready for this?) "count **all things** to be loss for the surpassing value of knowing Christ Jesus my Lord."

EXTREME Gratitude

You may be thinking, "You got that right. My divorce was a tremendous loss." Or, "My business failure and the resulting financial disaster was an immense loss."

No, hear Him. "Count all things to be loss *for the surpassing value of knowing* Christ Jesus, my Lord." If you are looking at the loss you experienced, and mourning it and grieving over it, you are still valuing what you lost. I still find myself doing this at times. Because of the debt we accumulated when I had cancer, we no longer were able to keep putting money back into the photography business to market it and grow it, or even really for all the day-to-day expenses. So, I "retired." There was no retirement income. Honestly, I just had to walk away from it and go to work for someone else, just to have a steady paycheck. There are times I would love to go back into photography. I enjoyed it. I'm good at it. However, in today's economy, it does not pay well. I know many well-established photographers who have left the industry as well. Most who are still in it, have some other source of income—a steady retirement check from another career, or a spouse with an income that covers most of their needs. So, starting over in photography is just not a wise option for me. There are times I "mourn" that loss. The job I went to was just a job for a paycheck. It was not something I enjoyed. My heart was not in it. It had no eternal value other than a rare moment when I got to share a little of Jesus with a co-worker or customer. There were times I found it very frustrating. However, my having that job was not an eternal problem either. I can mourn the loss of the photography business. I can grumble or grouse or feel sorry for myself because of my current job. Or, I can let go of it—lose it, as it were. I can trust God to use this, too, for my growth. I can see this as an opportunity to get to know Him better, to learn and grow.

Lose your loss. Let go of your hurts and frustrations. Count that loss itself, the experience of it, as loss, for the surpassing value of knowing Christ. Let your experiences, good or bad, gain or loss, result in your receiving the greater benefit of knowing

Him. Your experiences, good or bad, joyful or painful, are temporal. Their only eternal value or significance is when you let go of them and allow God to use them to reveal more of Himself through them.

No, I am not saying stifle your emotions. I am not saying it is a sin for you to grieve over a loss. You will. You are human. You need to grieve over things that hurt. Feel your hurt. But don't live there. Don't stay there forever. At some point, let your hurt cause you to let go of this world of temporary things a little more, and cling to Him. "Therefore we do not lose heart, but though our outer man is decaying, yet our inner man is being renewed day by day. For momentary, light affliction is producing for us an eternal weight of glory far beyond all comparison, while we look not at the things which are seen, but at the things which are not seen; for the things which are seen are temporal, but the things which are not seen are eternal" (2 Corinthians 4:16-18). Praise God that my hair is getting more gray. Several years ago I had to finally get reading glasses (now I'm up to bifocals). My knees bend just fine, but they don't straighten back out as easily as they used to. I know I'm not getting taller, but it seems like when I have to sit on the floor, or pick something up off the ground, it's further down there and back than it used to be. Hallelujah, this body is decaying so that I can let go of the temporal and receive an eternal weight of glory far beyond all comparison. "For I consider that the sufferings of this present time are not worthy to be compared with the glory that is to be revealed to us" (Romans 8:18).

If we will count both our gains and losses to be lost for the surpassing value of knowing Him, nothing the enemy throws at us can have a lasting effect on us. Instead, even the things the enemy throws at us will result in our knowing Christ, so that the results he was seeking to accomplish never happen. The work of the devil is made of no effect (Hebrews 2:14). This is the application of the cross to our life. This is being crucified to the world (Galatians 5:24).

EXTREME Gratitude

God is contending for the affection of His people. He loves us dearly, deeply, passionately, and He longs for us to love Him with the same fervor. But we love the world. We count everything except Him to be gain. We mouth the words from time to time, but do not yet truly mean it when we say, "I count all things loss for the surpassing value of knowing Him."

What you spend time with is what you value. What you treat with respect and tenderness is what you value. What you value, you say nice things about. (In other words, you praise.) What is worthy of being valued by you? What is more worthy of being valued by you than He is? "All things" are eclipsed by the surpassing value of knowing Him.

Paul was in prison when he wrote the letter to the Philippians (1:12-17). As a prisoner, what good did circumcision do him? What was the benefit of being descended from Benjamin? What good was there in being an "ideal Hebrew," a Pharisee, a zealous persecutor of the church? What did it matter that He was a strict, "righteous" legalist? None. He had suffered the loss of all things for the sake of Christ. He had nothing; no possessions; no home. All the education, all the past good things he had done, although they could not be taken away, were of no use.

Can you relate? Have you experienced some losses lately? Maybe you did not lose everything because someone took them from you and imprisoned you for being such a good Christian. But God is sovereign. He allowed you to lose all those things. Yes, He did allow that loved one to die. He did allow your spouse the freedom to choose to move out. He is willing to take the blame for your present situation because He is that comfortable with His sovereignty, and He sees the surpassing value of your having nothing to hold on to but Him.

We are talking about a God who has a song that He likes to sing about *you* (Zephaniah 3:17). He created you for fellowship with Himself. He desires that everything about your life be to the praise of the glory of His grace (Ephesians 1:12). He wants you to enjoy Him (Psalm 37:4). He is not trying to make you miserable and take all the pleasure out of your life. He is simply trying to help you stop settling for the meager pleasures this world offers, when you could have the much greater pleasure and joy in life that you can find only in Him.

"Settling." It is not only in the area of earthly pleasures that we settle for less than God desires for us and offers to us. It is also in the area of Christian living and lifestyle. We have so many plans, programs, and events. We don't know how just to be Christian. We think church is something we "go to" and that Christianity is the things we do. Instead of equipping the saints, the church manufactures what it calls a Christian life composed of classes, seminars, programs, and events. We are proclaiming religious activities instead of teaching people how to love God and live in His strength.

We proclaim God's standard in this area of life or that. We forget that God is "*Yahweh Nissi*," "The Lord My Banner" (or, "Standard"). He is the flag we follow into battle. He is the flag we raise to identify who we are. He is the flag we raise to proclaim victory and to claim conquered territory. We get so busy proclaiming His standard, that we forget that He Himself is our Standard. We want so much to be holy that we try to find all the things we need to do to be holy. Yet, in all our efforts we never make it. The only way for us to "be perfect as your Father in Heaven is perfect," to "be holy for I am holy," is to allow Him to be both *Yahweh Nissi*, "The Lord Our Standard," and *Yahweh M'Kaddesh*, "The Lord Who Sanctifies" (or "Makes Holy"). We settle for so much less than He desires for us when we seek to raise up a standard, and that standard is anything less than God Himself. "The chief thing is, not to know *what* God has said we must do, but that *God Himself* says it to us. It is not the law, and not the book, not the knowledge of what is right, that works obedience, but the personal influence of God and His living fellowship."[1]

Oh, do hear this, child of God. Your Father knows how to give good things to His children. Your Father longs to give good things to you. He craves the privilege of giving you great joy. He enjoys watching you open the presents He gives you. He takes great delight in giving you great delight. He has fun blessing you. How the Father's heart must break because His children do not believe He really loves them. How He must yearn to convince us He really wants only our good. In fact, in Hebrews 6:13-18, God swears that it is His fervent desire to bless us. Commenting on this Andrew Murray wrote:

> "Oh if we would but take time to tarry in the presence of this God and to listen to Him swearing to us that He will be faithful, surely we should fall down in confusion that we ever harbored for a moment the doubt, which thinks it possible that He may be untrue and not keep His word. Shall we not kneel and vow that by His grace, we will rather die than again make such a God a liar? ... In the Christian life, there is lack of steadfastness, of diligence, of perseverance. Of all the cause is simply—lack of faith. And of this again, the cause is—the lack of the knowledge of what God wills and is, of His purpose and power to bless most wonderfully, and of His faithfulness to carry out His purpose. It is to cure those evils; it is to tell His people that He will do anything to win their trust, and will do anything for them if they will trust Him, that God has taken His oath of faithfulness. ... And shall we not count it our most sacred duty, and our most blessed privilege, to honor God every day by a life of full and perfect trust?"[2]

"The lack of the knowledge of what He wills and is ..." echoes the words of Hebrews, "Without faith, it is impossible to please Him. For he that comes to God must believe that He is, and that He is a rewarder of those who seek Him." Without faith, it is impossible to please Him. For He that comes to God must believe that He is, and that He is a rewarder of those who seek

Him. He exists. He is. He is God—creator, sovereign, loving Father, eternal, righteous, holy, almighty, and so much more. **And**, He is a rewarder of those who seek Him. He is faithful, and worthy of our total trust and confidence. In Greek, the noun "faith" and the verb "believe" are from the same root word. It is unfortunate that we don't have a verb for faith in English. So, I will at times force it and use "faith" as a verb. "Believe" is just used too lightly. The significance of "must believe that He is" is too easily glossed over. God has given us six senses. With five of them we experience the physical world. God is a spiritual being and cannot be fully experienced with our five physical senses. To know Him requires faith. Faith is not a blind leap into the unknown. It is the sense by which we experience the spiritual. By faith we experience the spiritual just as we use sight to perceive light and hearing to perceive sound. To come to God we must believe, or "faith," first of all, that He is—in other words, that He exists, and that He exists as God—and second, that He is a rewarder of those who seek Him. If you do not believe that there is some merit in seeking Him, you won't do it. If you truly believe that He will respond to you, that He will allow Himself to be found by you, and that He will reward your efforts in a way that only God can, nothing will be able to hold you back from seeking Him, and knowing Him. If we would only see the surpassing value of knowing Him above all else, we would be at the beginning of always abiding in His presence, before His throne, face to face. If we could only grasp that His greatest gift is Himself, we would count all else to be rubbish, and we would gain Him (Phil. 3:8).

What a door that opens. "In those days ... I will cause a righteous Branch of David to spring forth; and He shall execute justice and righteousness on the earth. In those days Judah will be saved, and Jerusalem will dwell in safety; and this is the name by which she [Jerusalem] will be called: 'the Lord is our righteousness'" (Jeremiah 33:15-16). One fulfillment of the promise of a New Jerusalem is that we gain Christ Himself, and He is our dwelling place. **He** is our city, "The Lord is Our Righteousness." We are found "in Him, not having a righteousness of my own derived from the Law, but that which is through faith in Christ, the righteousness which comes from God on the basis of faith" (Philippians 3:9).

This process of counting all things loss is part of the process of crucifixion, whereby we die to the temporal and cling to the eternal. We die to righteousness of our own making, derived from Law, in order to live in the righteousness that is from Him based on faith. By being conformed to His death, we may know Him, and the power of His resurrection, and the fellowship of His sufferings.

Chapter 2

The Atoning Work of Christ

An Administration Suitable to the Fullness of Times

God has always wanted relationship with man. He walked with Adam in the garden. Adam, being the only human, was all of mankind. The first eleven chapters of Genesis tell of this relationship and how it was disrupted by man's sin. Through Adam, sin entered the world, and with sin, death.

Coming on the heels of the stories of the fall and corruption of mankind, through which all mankind died, losing the life of paradise is Abraham. In Abraham, God's thoughts regarding the redemption of mankind take somewhat of a new twist. He narrows the focus of redemption history to one select group, a chosen people. However, Abraham and Sarah have no children, and are too old to start. They were in effect dead to childbearing. Paul says Abraham was as good as dead and also refers to the deadness of Sarah's womb (Romans 4:19). Out of this death, God provided life, through the miraculous birth of Isaac. Not only was this birth significant in itself, but it was the beginning of the ancestry of the One through Whom "all the families of the earth will be blessed" (Genesis 12:3). Abraham became the father of Him who was before him, the path God chose to bring life back to mankind. In Abraham, God demonstrated that life always comes out of death.

This is the basis of the old covenant system of sacrifice. Considerable detail is given in the Old Testament to the entire system of sacrifices and tabernacle worship. The tabernacle is described from the inside out in Exodus 25-27. There is the ark of the covenant, topped by the mercy seat between two cherubim. There is the table of the *shewbread* that held the bread of the Presence in dishes of pure gold. There is the lampstand, hammered according to precise directions from a single piece of gold. The type of materials, colors, designs, and dimensions are laid out in detail.

The tabernacle was to be divided by a veil, separating the holy place from the holy of holies. The ark, with the mercy seat, was to be placed in the holy of holies. The table and the lampstand, along with an altar for burning incense, were in the holy place. An altar was placed in the courtyard for sacrifices. This altar was five cubits (about 90 inches) square, three cubits (about 48 inches) high. Each altar, the altar for incense and the altar of sacrifice, had a horn protruding from each of its four corners. Between the altar of sacrifice, in the courtyard, and the tent was a bronze laver, in which the priests were to wash their hands and feet before offering a sacrifice or entering the tent. The tabernacle was surrounded by walls, forming a courtyard enclosure, 100 cubits long on its north and south walls, and 50 cubits wide on its east and west walls with the gate in the east wall.

Much more detail is given in the Biblical account, and if you read in 1 Kings 6-7 and 2 Chronicles 3-5, you will see a similar account of the larger and not so portable versions of these things that went into the temple which Solomon built. Make a commitment to yourself to read these accounts and to research the meaning of some of the details of art, design, and color that went into the tabernacle and the temple. For now, let's expound on what we have here.

The sacrifice was the core of the old covenant system of worship. By it, sins were forgiven, and purification was made. The priests were to "bring the bull to the doorway of the tent of meeting before the Lord, and he shall lay his hand on the head of the bull, and slay the bull before the Lord. Then the anointed priest is to take some of the blood of the bull and bring it to the tent of meeting, and the priest shall dip his finger in the blood and sprinkle some of the blood seven times before the Lord, in front of the veil of the sanctuary. The priest shall also put some of the blood on the horns of the altar of fragrant incense which is before the Lord in the tent of meeting; and all the blood of the bull he shall pour out at the base of the altar of burnt offering which is at the doorway of the tent of meeting" (Leviticus 4:3-7).

These things are wondrous in their symbolism. Yet, as long as that earthly tabernacle was standing, the way into the holiest was not disclosed (Hebrews 9:8). Only the high priest, and he only once a year, could come into the holy of holies, the dwelling place of God. Even so, the gifts and sacrifices offered through this system could not make the worshiper perfect in conscience. If they could, then the average person could enter with confidence into the holy of holies (1 John 3:21). But the old covenant regulations had to do with food and drink and various washings, regulations for the body imposed until a time of reformation (Hebrews 9:10-11). These things had to be repeated over and over. Their effect did not last. The whole system was imperfect. Something more was needed. And in the fullness of time, or at the proper time, God summed up all things in Christ, things in the heavens and things upon the earth (Ephesians 1:10).

Jesus replaced the repetitious system with a once for all system. The writer of Hebrews calls the old system weak and useless because it makes nothing perfect, pointing us to a better hope and a better covenant enacted on better promises (Hebrews 7:18-19, 8:6). Jesus entered through a greater and more perfect tabernacle, through His blood, entering the holy place once for all, having obtained eternal redemption (Hebrews 9:11-12). Now if the blood of bulls and goats was accepted by God for the sanctifying of the flesh of the worshipers under the old covenant, **"how much more will the blood of Christ ... cleanse your conscience from dead works to serve the living God?"** (Hebrews 9:13-14).

Now, let's go back to the temple/tabernacle and take a closer look that will really demonstrate this. In Exodus 25, God gave Moses the instructions for the Holy of Holies, the innermost part of the tabernacle, including the Ark of the Covenant. On top of the ark, he was to build a seat, like a bench. The Hebrew word is *capporeth*. It was to be 3½ cubits long and 1½ cubits wide (figuring a cubit at about 18" that would be 45" x 27") and was called the mercy seat. At each end of it, was a cherubim. The whole assembly of bench and cherubim was to be covered with gold as one piece. Each of the cherubim was to face inward, looking at the mercy seat. The wings of the cherubim swept inward, toward one another, over the mercy seat, and touching wingtips. God told Moses, "And there I will meet with you; and from above the mercy seat, from between the two cherubim which are upon the ark of the testimony, I will speak to you about all that I will give you in commandment for the sons of Israel" (Exodus 25:22).

In addition, on the annual day of atonement, the high priest would sacrifice a bull as a sin offering and a ram as a burnt offering for himself. In addition, he was to take from the congregation two male goats for a sin offering and a ram for a burnt offering for the people. Of the two goats, he was to cast lots and thereby select one of the goats for the sacrifice. The other goat was the "scapegoat," and was presented alive before the Lord, and was then released into the wilderness. When the priest entered the Holy of Holies, he was to take the blood of the bull and sprinkle it with his finger on the east end of the mercy seat and in front of the mercy seat. Then he was to take the blood of the goat, the sin offering for the people, and sprinkle it on and in front of the mercy seat.

In the Septuagint, the Greek translation of the Hebrew Old Testament, the word *capporeth* is always translated by the Greek word *"hilasterion."* In the Greek, the word means "propitiation." It's the word used in Romans 3:25 referring to Jesus as the one "whom God displayed publicly as a propitiation in His blood through faith."

If you look up propitiation in a lexicon, you will also find other big, religious-sounding words—like expiation, conciliation, redemption, and justification. If you look them up in Webster's dictionary, you'll find the concept of most have to do with an attempt to please God, to make atonement, find forgiveness, restore peace or friendship with God.

Let these scriptures sink in for a moment. First, in Exodus and Leviticus, the scriptures about the mercy seat make God

EXTREME Gratitude

the "prime mover." **He is the One who told Moses to make the mercy seat.** In other words, He is the One who chose to make a way and chose the way to reconcile man to Himself. He acted first. It wasn't about man trying to find a way to appease God. God provided a way for man to find forgiveness and to be reconciled to God.

Consider Romans 3:25. God took on flesh and blood in the person of His Son, the Messiah, Jesus. Jesus became the propitiation, the Mercy Seat. And it wasn't with the blood of bulls or rams or goats, but through His blood and because of the incredible "forbearance (patience) of God that He passed over the sins previously committed." In Jesus is the Mercy Seat, the Blood, the Passover. In Jesus is redemption, reconciliation, propitiation, atonement, forgiveness, salvation. It is **by His doing**. "Apart from the Law the righteousness of God has been manifested, being witnessed by the Law and the Prophets, even the righteousness of God through faith in Jesus Christ for all those who believe; for there is no distinction; for all have sinned and come short of the glory of God, being justified as a gift by His grace through the redemption which is in Christ Jesus; whom God displayed publicly as a propitiation in His blood through faith, to demonstrate His righteousness, because in the forbearance of God He passed over the sins previously committed" (Romans 3:21-25). Jesus did not do away with the Law. He fulfilled it.

The new covenant is Jesus on the altar of sacrifice once for all (instead of animals in frequent sacrifices, including the annual day of atonement). Under the old covenant, the animal was sacrificed in front of the people, outside the tent of meeting. Jesus was taken to a hillside for public execution so all for whom atonement was being made could see. The blood of the animal sacrifice was taken into the tent of meeting and sprinkled before the veil and upon the four horns of the altar of incense. Jesus hung before the multitudes, bleeding from four points, His head, His hands, and His feet, and turned the cross into an altar of incense as He interceded for His executioners. The remainder of the blood of the animal sacrifice was poured out at the base of the altar of sacrifice before the people, even as Jesus' blood was poured out at the foot of His cross. The veil hung in the temple to separate the holy place in which the priests ministered from the holy of holies in which the glory of God dwelled and into which the high priest alone could enter once a year and only with the proper preparation and sacrifices. Under the new covenant, "we have confidence to enter the holy place by the blood of Jesus, by a new and living way which He inaugurated for us through the veil, that is, His flesh" (Hebrews 10:19-20). Through His blood, He cleansed us for entering in, and through the tearing of His flesh, He tore open the veil of the temple and opened a new and living way for us to enter into the very presence of the living God.

If all this talk of blood is a bit much for you because of your upbringing, or because of deep hurts in your heart resulting from your past sins, or from pains inflicted on you through abuse at the hands of another, then let Him wash you with water now. In the old covenant, the priests washed with water. In the new, the water poured from Jesus' own body when His side was pierced. He will cleanse you to enter into the holy place, to experience the light of His lampstand (Colossians 1:12-13), to feed on the bread of His presence (John 6:48-58), and to communicate with Him at the altar of incense.

Please, dear friend, do not be satisfied to remain in the outer court of the tabernacle, as the Israelites did while the priests entered on their behalf. He hears your prayer, "Deliver me from bloodguiltiness," and He bids you enter into the holy of holies, to draw near to Him, "having our hearts sprinkled clean from an evil conscience and our bodies washed with pure water" (Hebrews 4:16; 10:22b) by means of an eternal, once for all redemption. He hears your prayer, "Hide Your face from my sins," and when He turned His back on His Son, prompting Him to cry out, "My God, why have You forsaken Me?", He was turning His back and hiding His face from your sins and mine.

This is what you have sung about for years:

> *Rock of Ages, cleft for me,*
> *Let me hide myself in Thee.*[1]

The "Rock of Ages" is Jesus, isn't it? What is a "cleft"? It is a somewhat archaic word for a hole or crag. What cleft is there in the life of Christ other than the cross?

If by chance you are reading this, and you are not a Christian, this is where you get in to a new life with Christ. You must give up all the things you are doing to make your life comfortable, to find peace, to please God, and make yourself acceptable. Becoming a Christian is not something you do by your self-effort. You stop your efforts and find the rest for which you are looking by trusting that what Jesus did was sufficient to meet your needs and make you clean and whole, to straighten out the mess you and others have made of your life, and to make you acceptable to God.

If you are a Christian, then this is how you go on in the Christian life. Because the way you get in is the way you go on.

Chapter 3

Corn Kernel Christianity

The Way You Get In Is the Way You Go On

"Oh, man! I am dying inside! Why does this hurt so much. Can't God see what I'm going through? Why doesn't He put an end to this?"

John 12:24 says:

> *"Unless a grain of wheat falls into the earth and dies, it remains alone, but if it dies, it brings forth much fruit."*

"O, thanks a lot. Just what I needed, another Christian cliché. Do you have any more pat answers that don't relate at all to what I'm going through, and certainly don't help stop my hurting? Why don't you quote Romans 8:28 while you're at it?"

It is time we learned that God's word does contain very relevant answers to life's hurts. And one of the most relevant is the lesson of the seed.

My dad grew up in rural Pennsylvania in the foothills of the Allegheny Mountains. The house, as I remember it, sat on about an acre of cleared land, surrounded by woods. On one side was a steep hill. At the top of the hill was a meadow. Dad said when he was a boy, his grandfather and father farmed that land. Dad applied this education in planting and cultivating his back yard garden when I was growing up. Our house sat on an acre of land, and Dad's garden was about the size of the entire back yard of many modern city lots. When he planted his corn, he put four seeds in each hole. One day while helping him, I asked him why. It was a lesson he learned from his dad, and he explained it to me with a poem passed down from his granddad:

*One for the worm,
and one for the crow;
One to rot,
and one to grow.*

Look back at John 12:24. Which of these four seeds would be the one that falls into the ground and dies in order to bring forth much fruit? Obviously, the one for the worm and the one for the crow are taken out of the picture. Although we might tend to think of rotting as resulting from death, the one that rots obviously does not grow either. That only leaves one. So how does it grow if it dies? And if it dies, why doesn't it rot?

If you pull up the corn stalk, will the kernel from which it grew still be there? What happened to it? You are holding it in your hand. Ears of corn will not grow on the corn kernel itself. It must cease to be a seed and become a stalk. It must "die" to being a seed in order to become the corn stalk on which more ears can be produced.

As we experience the most difficult and painful experiences of our lives, we often think we are going through "Hell on earth." We compare our hurt to the pain of dying. We think of the experience in terms of bearing our cross, often in mournful resignation declaring, "This must be 'my cross to bear.'"

No! Your cross is His cross. The painful experience you are going through is not your cross. It is a painful experience that you are going through. It relates to the cross of Jesus in your life only as it points out to you to what extent and in what areas of your life you are operating in your strength, not depending on Him, and stubbornly trying to maintain control of your life.

Now, before I push you too far, let's back off and approach this from a different angle that will help ensure that we are putting this in terms we can both understand.

In January 1975, I entered Southwestern Baptist Theological Seminary in Fort Worth. Among my classes that first semester was a required course called "Missionary Preparations." Dr. Cal Guy taught the practical aspects of missions—mission procedures, methods, and such. Dr. Jack Gray taught spiritual preparations for missions, with sessions on basic spiritual growth, prayer, the Holy Spirit. No other class has ever had the impact on me that this one did. Many things were shared by both professors that have had a lasting influence. The most profound was this simple phrase that Dr. Gray used frequently: "The way you get in is the way you go on."

What does it mean? Is it scriptural? I guarantee it is far, far more than just a trite cliché. Look at Colossians 2:6. It reads:

> *"Therefore, as you have received Christ Jesus, so walk in Him."*

Do you see it? As (in the manner) you have received Him, so (in the same manner) walk. The way you received Him is the way you walk. The way you get in is the way you go on.

What does that mean? You'll be amazed at how profound this is. It is really awesome. Are you ready? It means this: **As** you received Christ Jesus, so walk in Him. How did you receive Him? Most of us, at the time of our salvation, did not fully understand all the dynamics involved. So, let's consider it together.

Is it not true that you had to reach the place where you realized that you did not and **could not** please God? You needed a savior because you could not save yourself. Jesus had done **everything** (see Chapter 2) necessary to secure your salvation. You ceased from all your efforts to save yourself and make yourself pleasing to Him, and you rested in what Jesus had accomplished for you. The way you get in is the way you go on.

At the moment of your salvation, you went to the cross. It was a place of death. Not Christ's death only, though. According to Paul in Romans 6, Colossians 3, Philippians 3, and 2 Corinthians 4, you shared in His death. This is part of the "ceasing from your efforts." A dead man does not work. The way you get in is the way you go on.

Go to the cross daily. The message of the cross is the power of God to us who are being saved (1 Corinthians 1:18). What is the message of the cross? Is it not death? The way you get in is the way you go on. This is what Jesus meant when He said, "If anyone wishes to come after Me, he must deny himself, take up his cross daily, and follow me" (Luke 9:23). Daily! The way you get in is the way you go on.

"For by grace you have been saved through faith; and that not of yourself, it is the gift of God; not as a result of works, so that no one may boast" (Ephesians 2:8-9). By grace through faith! The way you get in is the way you go on. So, Paul wrote the book of Galatians to stress that the Christian walk is a walk of grace and faith. "I am amazed that you are so quickly deserting Him who called you **by the grace of Christ**. ... You have been severed from Christ, you who are seeking to be justified by law; **you have fallen from grace**" (Galatians 1:6, 5:4). Please note, this says "fallen from grace," not "fallen from salvation."

The word translated "severed from" is more literally translated "made of no effect" or "non-work." When you work with a computer, you can type for hours and hours to accomplish a task, whether it is using existing software, or writing your program. However, if you do not "save" your work on a disk when you shut off the computer, all your work will be without result, i.e., as if it were never done.

As a believer, when you seek to be justified by the law—to live by rules and self-effort apart from grace, your efforts are made of no effect. All your efforts are "non-works," without results.

Do you feel powerless in your walk with the Lord? Bless His name; you are powerless! Quit trying to do God's work in your strength. Glory in your weakness. Rejoice in it. There is no better place in all the world for you to be than in absolute dependence upon the Father. So depend on Him. Rest in Him. Walk in the grace that saved you. You will very likely find yourself doing the same work you are doing now, but in His strength and ability rather than your own. It will be a work characterized by inner peace, not by emotional turmoil, striving, and burnout. And that is all the difference in the world. Think about your abilities, the things you are capable of doing. Now, think about the things God is capable of doing, His abilities. Now, whose ability would you rather operate in, yours or His?

What is the explosive potential of a stick of dynamite? Can you have your dynamite and your explosion, too? The dynamite must cease to be in order for the explosive power to be released. What about a nuclear explosion? Is it not accomplished by splitting an atom? The atom must cease to be as it was in order for the explosive force to be released. And "the message of the cross ... to us who are being saved, it is the power ["dunamis" is the Greek word] of God."

Romans 6:6 says that "our old self was crucified with Him, that our body of sin might be done away with." The words "done away with" are the translation of the same word as "severed from" in Galatians 5:4. Our old nature was crucified with Christ, so that sin within our flesh might be rendered powerless. The tendency of our flesh toward its old sin patterns is made of no effect by the cross.

Hebrews 2:14 says that Jesus took on flesh and blood and went to the cross so that "through death He might render powerless him who had the power of death, that is the devil." Again, the same word appears in the Greek. "Rendered powerless" means "made of no effect." Through the Cross of Jesus, Satan is made of no effect.

Do you see the pattern? The flesh is rendered powerless by the cross. Satan is, too. You, however, are rendered of no effect when you seek to be justified by law and get away from the cross, God's gracious provision for your getting in and your going on. Or, as we read in 1 Corinthians 1:18: "The word of the cross is to ... us who are being saved ... the power of God." The word translated power is "dunamis." It is where we get our word dynamite, but its true meaning is "the inherent ability." The word, or message, of the cross, is death. The result is that with you "out of the way" as it were, the inherent ability of God, what He is "naturally" capable of doing, because He is God, is turned loose in you. We are "always carrying about in the body the dying of Jesus, so that the life of Jesus also may be manifested in our body" (2 Corinthians 4:10). As you go to the cross and let it make your flesh and your enemy, Satan, of no effect, and as you cease from your efforts to live by the law and self-effort for your justification, the ability of God Himself is turned loose in you, just as the life of Jesus is manifested in you.

The whole point is we must be dependent on the Father. We have to depend on Him to apply the cross to our life. Just as Jesus could have come down from the cross, He could just as easily, miraculously, have ascended the cross. But He came as a lamb to the slaughter. "Just as it is written, 'For Your sake we are being put to death all day long; we were considered as sheep to be slaughtered'" (Romans 8:36; Psalm 44:22). The lamb was taken to the altar and was killed. It did not volunteer. It was led. Jesus came as a lamb to the slaughter, not only in His innocence but also in His yieldedness. He did not walk up to the cross and climb up and nail Himself to it. He was led. He was crucified. It was done to Him. Likewise, we do not nobly go and jump upon the altar of self-sacrifice. We, too, are to be yielded to the hand of the One Who is daily renewing us after the image of Him that created our new nature (Colossians 3:10).

We are to "put on" the traits of the new man. How do we do that? What is the new man? The new man is the one who has died and whose life is hid with Christ in God (Colossians 3:3). He is the one who is crucified, yet lives, yet doesn't live, but Christ lives in him (Galatians 2:20). The way you put him on is the way you got in—total dependence that He Who began a good work in you is able to complete that work.

You got in by ceasing from your efforts and resting in what He did on your behalf. You go on the same way. You got in through the cross, you go on by the cross. You got in by grace through faith; you go on by grace through faith. You could not save yourself, and you cannot sanctify yourself! In fact, your sanctification is not your responsibility. "For I am confident of this very thing, that **He that began a good work in you will**

perfect it until the day of Christ Jesus" (Philippians 1:6). "For it is God who is at work in you **both** to will **and to work** for His good pleasure" (Philippians 2:13).

Some will ask, "What about faith? Isn't that doing something; putting faith in God?" No, even faith is the gift of God, so "no one may boast" (Ephesians 2:8-10). Furthermore, faith is trust, dependence. Faith is rest, a ceasing from work. We are to yield in total dependence to our loving, holy God and rest in His grace to accomplish His purposes in us.

Have you ever felt like your walk with the Lord is best symbolized by an up-and-down, rollercoaster graph? You feel like you do so well for a while. You are growing in the Lord. Then you backslide. Eventually, you get turned around and begin growing again, only to go through the same process over and over. Sound familiar?

Consider this. A tree grows during the spring time, three months out of the year. The remainder of the year is spent solidifying that growth. God does no less with us. He is the one responsible for our growth. He knows we can only handle so much at one time. He grows us. Then when He deems best, He **stops the growth**, putting it on hold and allowing us to solidify in what we have just learned. The heat and drought of summer, the storms and dying and stripping bare of autumn, and the coldness and death of winter mature us and make the new growth a vital part of us. Then He can add to it the next season of growth. If we really believe that "He who began a good work in you will complete it", then when the period of fast growth suddenly comes to an end, we will not panic. We will know that He is still in control. We will trust Him and rest in Him.

Do not despair if more of your life seems to be spent in conformity to His death than in the power of His resurrection. Actually, it is the power of resurrection that gets us through the seasons of death. The way of death is the way of life. Look at the sequence of Philippians 3:10-11: "That I may know Him, and the power of His resurrection and the fellowship of His sufferings, being conformed to His death; in order that I may attain to the resurrection from the dead." Knowing Him and the power of His resurrection leads to, not from, the fellowship of His sufferings, and being conformed to His death. Yet this, in turn, leads to resurrection and the life side of the cross. It is "**always** carrying about in the body the dying of Jesus, that the life of Jesus also may be manifested in our body" (2 Corinthians 4:10).

Let's look one more time at the example of the seed. Romans 6:3-5 speaks of our being buried with Christ in His death. This is the ground of our growth. "Greater love has no one than this, that one lay down his life for his friends" (John 15:13). The death of Christ is the love into which we are rooted and grounded (Ephesians 3:19). "We might also use the figure once referred to by the Rev. Andrew Murray, when he spoke of the acorn striking its roots into the ground, whilst the life sprang up into an oak."[1] Life always comes out of death. As the acorn dies to being a seed and begins sending its roots deep into the soil, it draws life from the soil which goes into the growing up of the tree above ground. As the tree continues to abide in the soil, it continues to draw life from the soil and continues to grow large and strong. It is a long slow process to grow an oak tree, but the results are worth it. The oak is one of the largest and strongest trees. It is hardy and healthy, not easily damaged or diseased. A willow or cottonwood may grow more quickly, but they are weaker, more susceptible to disease and shorter-lived. "It is as we abide in the ground of His death by faith that we strike the roots of faith deep down into Him, like a planted acorn, and thus His life springs up in us into 'newness of life'; 'resurrection life'; the ascension life within the veil."[2] This is how we become "oaks of righteousness, the planting of the Lord, that He may be glorified" (Isaiah 61:3).

When I first began to study spiritual growth, one of the first resources I turned to was Miles Stanford's Principles of Spiritual Growth (also titled The Green Letters). In it, Stanford delineates a list of separate principles of growth. One of the principles was "appropriation," which states that as you learn what is already yours in Christ, and as you experience a practical need, you will appropriate, or receive from Him what He has already done to meet that need. As I read this book and others dealing with the Christian life and growth, I began "appropriating" everything in sight. I was starving for more of the Lord. His response was in effect, "You asked for it, so I'm going to give you what you're requesting in such a way that you will know that I heard your prayer."

My life suddenly seemed to get even more complicated and more painful than it already was. What God was pouring into my life had multiple effects. First, He sustained me through a time of great crisis. Second, contrasted to the depth of hurt and confusion in my life, He showed me how suffering can be our greatest teacher. Third, He showed me that I could not handle, all at once, all that I was asking Him to teach me. Finally, He convinced me that my growth—what I was to learn at a given time, the teaching method, and the pace at which He would teach me—is His responsibility.

This is the daily cross. This is always carrying about in the body the dying of Jesus. It is coming to an end of all your efforts to take responsibility for your growth away from the Lord, who began it. It is resting in Him who is at work both to will and to work for His good pleasure. It is trusting that the God who is, is a willing and faithful rewarder of those who seek Him.

All this is foretold by the prophet Ezekiel:

> *And my servant David will be king over them,*
> *and they will all have one shepherd; and they will walk*
> *in My ordinances, and keep My statutes, and observe them*
> *… and will set My sanctuary in their midst forever.*
> *My dwelling place also will be with them; and I will be*
> *their God, and they will be My people. And the nations will*
> *know that I am the Lord who sanctifies Israel when*
> *My sanctuary is in their midst forever.*
> Ezekiel 37:24-28

Rick Carr

As further proof that He is the one responsible for our growth, He has given the Sabbath rest as proof that He is the one who sanctifies.

Chapter 4

The Sabbath Rest

"For He is our God, and we are the people of His pasture and the sheep of His hand. Today, if you would hear His voice, do not harden your hearts, as at Meribah, as in the day of Massah in the wilderness, 'When your fathers tested Me, they tried Me, though they had seen My work. For forty years, I loathed that generation and said they are a people who err in their heart, and they do not know My ways. Therefore, I swore in My anger, truly they shall not enter into My rest.'"

Psalm 95:7-11

The writer of Hebrews quotes this passage in Hebrews 3:7-11 to set the stage for a significant lesson on Sabbath Rest.

In verse 12, he begins one of the four "warning" passages in Hebrews, saying, "Take care, brethren, that there not be in any one of you an evil, unbelieving heart that falls away from the living God." I mentioned earlier that the Greek verb we translate "believe" is the verb form of the noun "faith." It works the same in reverse. "Unbelief" translates the Greek word "*apistis*"—"a" meaning "not" and "*pistis*," meaning faith. It's "unfaith." It's a heart without faith that falls away from God. It is evil to not faith God. It is sinful, and sin is deceitful. It leads away from God, and to further sin (see Romans 1:21 and following). It results in a hardened heart. So the writer urges us to encourage one another, quoting from the Psalms, "Today," saying we are partakers of Christ if we hold fast the assurance we began with, firm until the end. We are partakers of Him who took on flesh and yet remained sinless. We are urged to hold fast, to endure because it is a day to day experience. Every day is "today." He further points out that the Psalmist put his "Today" in the context of their Hebrew ancestors testing or "provoking" God in the wilderness. All those who came out of Egypt with Moses sinned against God and died in the wilderness without entering the Promised Land.

Verses 18-19 bring home the story and set the stage for what is to come. Verse 18: "And to whom did He swear that they would not enter His rest, but to those who were disobedient?" Then in verse 19: "So we see that they were not able to enter because of unbelief." So was it disobedience or unbelief? Or are they synonymous? If not synonymous, they are certainly interrelated. A lack of faith (unbelief) is evil. It is the basis, the foundation, the source of all our sin. When you sin, it is because at that point in your life, at least in relation to the decision you are making, you do not trust (or "faith") God. You do not believe He is a rewarder, and you are not allowing Him to be God in that area of your life. You are falling away from the living God.

This is where we win or lose. This is where Adam and Eve failed in the garden. They were created in the image of God. They walked and talked with Him in an eternal kind of fellowship. God told them, "From any tree of the garden you may freely eat; but from the tree of the knowledge of good and evil you shall not eat, for in the day that you eat from it you will surely die" (Genesis 2:16-17). The deceiver came and raised a question, "Indeed, has God said, 'You shall not eat from any tree of the garden?'" The woman replied, "From the fruit of the trees of the garden we may eat; but from the fruit of the tree which is in the middle of the garden, God has said, 'You shall not eat from it or touch it, or you will die.'" She added, "or touch it." She was already a little unsure of the original instructions. The serpent pressed the issue: "You surely will not die! For God knows that in the day you eat from it your eyes will be opened, and you will be like God, knowing good and evil." (Genesis 3:1-5). "You will be like God." What an offer?! Right? However, according to Genesis 1:27, God had created them in His image from the beginning. How much more "like God" can you be? It was their doubt, their lack of faith, their disbelief, that resulted in their act of disobedience. That has been the sin of man ever since.

The result of disobedience (or sin), the result of not having faith, is not entering into His rest. Obviously, the "rest" that was denied to the Hebrews in the wilderness was entering the land of promise. Or was it? The warning continues into Hebrews 4. "Therefore, let us fear if, while a promise remains of entering His rest, anyone of you may seem to have come short of it." "A promise remains." It remained for the first century Christians, and it remains for us today. Just as they, we have had the good news preached to us. It did not profit the Hebrew forefathers, because they did not unite the word with faith. They did not believe. Faith is the key to making the Word work in our hearts and thereby entering rest.

If we believe (faith), we enter rest, just as surely as He denied them rest, although His works were finished from the foundation of the world" (vs. 3). Verse 4 points to God's own "rest" on the seventh day as the foundation for the principle of rest. It isn't all about a geographical land. It is a spiritual condition.

In verse 5, the writer indicates the rest denied the Hebrews in the wilderness was a similar type of rest—not just geographical, but like God's rest. Okay, let this soak in. This is getting exciting. There **is** a rest that remains **for us**. God created the world in six days. However, Hebrews 4:1-11, would suggest that in the spiritual realm, the most real realm of all, He is still in the seventh day. Since we are bound to space and time, He works with us in this context to work out His will in the world.

Nonetheless, His works were finished from the foundation of the world. What does this mean for us? It means our salvation was secured from the foundation of the world. "He chose us in Him before the foundation of the world" (Ephesians 1:4). It means everything needed for us to be "holy and blameless before Him" (same verse) was done before the foundation of the world. All our prayers were answered before the foundation of the world. "Your Father knows what you need before you ask Him" (Matthew 6:8). "All things for which you pray and ask, believe that you have received them [already], and they shall be granted you" (Mark 11:24).

What God has accomplished in the reality of eternity, enters our space and time reality when we, by faith, believe that we have received it.[1] This is true of our salvation and our sanctification. Exodus 31:13 "But as for you, speak to the sons of Israel, saying, 'You shall surely observe My sabbaths; for this is a sign between Me and you throughout your generations, that you may know that I am the Lord who sanctifies you.'" The Sabbath is given as a reminder that God is the one who sanctifies. Our responsibility is to quit trying to sanctify ourselves and rest in the One who alone is able to make us holy and blameless and righteous.

The Hebrews may not have entered into it because of faithless disobedience, but it is available to us today. David, writing long after the time of Moses in the wilderness, says, "Today if you hear His voice, do not harden your hearts." If he was referring to Joshua's taking the people into Canaan as entering into rest, why would David, centuries later, say "today?" (Hebrews 4:6-8). That "today," is for us, too. We are partakers of Christ, holding fast our assurance day by day, from beginning to end.

Verses 9-10 spell it out unequivocally: "So there remains a Sabbath rest for the people of God. For the one who has entered His rest has himself also rested from his works, as God did from His." The Sabbath Rest for New Testament believers is ceasing from our works and resting in the finished work of Christ on our behalf. The way you get in is the way you go. You got in by resting in—faithing—the finished work of Christ on your behalf for your salvation. You go on by resting in—faithing—the finished work of God for your daily life and sanctification.

There is no point in struggling with anything other than the struggle (wearisome labor) to rest. The Greek word most often translated "labor" in the New Testament carries with it the idea of a wearisome struggle, a tiresome effort. It appears frequently. Paul proclaims, "and for this purpose, I labor, striving according to His power, which mightily works within me" (Colossians

1:29). He says, "But by the grace of God I am what I am, and His grace toward me did not prove vain; but I labored even more than all of them, yet not I, but the *grace of God* with me" (1 Corinthians 15:10) (Italics mine). The list goes on: verses that tell us we labor; but we don't; God does. However, there seems to be one significant exception. There is one challenge to labor that is not qualified by saying it is in fact, God's grace or God's power that actually does the work. Hebrews 4:11 challenges us to "labor to enter that rest." We **are** exhorted to labor to the point of wearisome struggle to rest. What a glorious paradox!

There is a rest that remains to the people of God. It is entered by ceasing from your efforts and resting in His (Hebrews 4:9-10), for He is at work both to will and to work for His good pleasure (Philippians 2:13). This is the most difficult challenge facing the contemporary Christian. Our culture, probably more than any in history, demands action. The humanistic influences of this century demand we work hard, be all we can be, do all we can do, in our own power. The emphasis on competitiveness causes us to repel at the idea of not pouring all our strength into achieving our goals. Scripture tells us to strive in His strength. This is hard for us. It takes significant effort not to do all we can do and let God do the rest. We are called to let Him be all. This is a struggle. But it is the only legitimate struggle for the Christian. If you are struggling with anything else, you are not resting. If you are struggling with finances, your spouse, your teenager, your job, the drivers who are hogging the highway, with illness, with temptation, or anything else, you are not resting. I have to admit, I struggled with this throughout my cancer treatment. Being diagnosed with cancer was one of the factors that triggered my desire to finally pursue finding a publisher. As I mentioned earlier, when I received the diagnosis of "squamous cell carcinoma" in a lymph gland in my neck I realized that if all the things I had shared through the years and put into this manuscript were true, I had better live them. This would be a time like no other in my life to apply these truths. I was right. The very nature and harshness of the treatment makes it hard not to focus on how your body feels. You are constantly physically fatigued as your body uses all its energy to not only fight the disease, but to recover from the treatment. You feel miserable, and it is hard to not struggle with it. It is hard to rest and not be discouraged. I found that when I applied these truths I felt better and recovered more quickly. The doctors described my response to treatment and my progress as "remarkable." What's remarkable is the power of God's word when combined with faith.

Between the economy and the medical bills during my cancer experience and my inability to keep up with my work, my photography business and our finances took quite a hit as well. Instead of being a rebuilding year, the next year was a year of frustration. I was amazed at how difficult it was to do many of the things that used to be so easy. Plus, there was car trouble, needed home repairs, and our daughter and her family were sent to Germany with the Army. In other words, there was life. After finding the value of faith and resting in the Lord in the face of cancer, I had to find it in the face of mundane, every day, life experience. And, it was every bit as much of a struggle.

Hebrews 4:12 declares: "The word of God is living and active and sharper than any two-edged sword …." This same word *(logos)* of God became flesh and dwelt among us (John 1:14). The *logos* of God is the Lord Jesus Christ. He sees to the very core of our being—"the division of soul and spirit, of both joints and marrow … the thoughts and intentions of the heart." Nothing is hidden from Him.

The Sabbath that remains for us definitely is not about a day of the week. This is why Jesus repeatedly healed on the Sabbath. To the Jews, this was "work" and violated the Law. To Jesus, it was a proper use of the Sabbath. "Is it lawful to do good or harm … save a life or kill?" (Mark 3:4). Jesus had no problem with His disciples picking and eating grain as they walked through a field on the Sabbath. To the Jews, this was work and violated the Sabbath Law. Jesus said, "The Sabbath was made for man, not man for the Sabbath. The Son of Man is Lord even of the Sabbath" (Mark 2:27-28). The Sabbath is for our benefit, not to dominate us. He is Lord of men, and Lord of the Sabbath. It is vital that we make knowing Him (not following the letter of the law for the sake of doing so) our top priority.

Therefore, because the one with whom we have to do can see all; because we are partakers of Him who took on flesh, faced temptation and remained sinless; because He is our great high priest we are urged to hold fast our confession and to draw near with confidence to the throne of grace in order to receive mercy and find grace.

The struggle to rest is a vital struggle for the Christian and not to be taken lightly. God takes the Sabbath rest very seriously.

We are introduced to the Sabbath Rest in Genesis 2:2-3, "And by the seventh day God completed His work which He had done; and he rested on the seventh day from all His work which He had done. Then God blessed the seventh day and sanctified it because in it He rested from all His work which God had created and made." Then in Exodus 20:8-11, the law is laid forth:

> *"Remember the sabbath day, to keep it holy. Six days you shall labor and do all your work, but the seventh day is a sabbath of the Lord your God; in it, you shall not do any work, you or your son or your daughter, your male or your female servant or your cattle or your sojourner who stays with you. For in six days, the Lord made the heavens and the earth, the sea and all that is in them, and rested on the seventh day; therefore, the Lord blessed the sabbath day and made it holy."*

Leviticus 25 sets forth the law regarding the Sabbatical year and the Year of Jubilee.

> "When you come into the land which I shall give you, then the land shall have a sabbath to the Lord. Six years you shall sow your field, and six years you shall prune your vineyard and gather in its crop, but during the seventh year the land shall have a sabbath rest, a sabbath to the Lord; you shall not sow your field nor prune your vineyard. Your harvest's aftergrowth you shall not reap, and your grapes of untrimmed vines you shall not gather; the land shall have a sabbatical year."

Now look at the story of the fall of Judah in 2 Chronicles 36:

> "Zedekiah was twenty-one years old when he became king, and he reigned eleven years in Jerusalem. And he did evil in the sight of the Lord his God. ... Therefore, He brought up against them the king of the Chaldeans who slew their young men with the sword in the house of their sanctuary, and had no compassion on young man or virgin, old man or infirm; He gave them all into his hand. And all of the house of the Lord, and the treasures of the king and of his officers, he brought them all to Babylon. Then they burned the house of God, and broke down the wall of Jerusalem and burned all its fortified buildings with fire, and destroyed all its valuable articles. And those who had escaped from the sword he carried away to Babylon; and they were servants to him and to his sons until the rule of the kingdom of Persia, to fulfill the word of the Lord by the mouth of Jeremiah, **until the land had enjoyed its sabbaths. All the days of its desolation it kept sabbath until seventy years were complete**" (emphasis mine).

Friend, God is very serious about the sabbath. We all need a break sometimes. From time to time, we need to stop working. Our failure to do so is responsible for numerous heart attacks, ulcers, and other both mental and physical maladies. Even more, it is the cause of much spiritual failure. We are body, soul, and spirit. Our bodies and our minds tell us when we need to rest physically and mentally, and if we do not listen, they break down and quit working in spite of us until they have "enjoyed their sabbaths." Unfortunately, we seem quite able to continue indefinitely spiritually. We explain our spiritual breakdowns and failures as just a part of life and growth. We convince ourselves we have no option but to sin. It is just the way we are and will be until we get to heaven.

I believe our real problem has more to do with our definition of sin. The biography of Andrew Murray contains a letter he wrote to his church regarding divine healing, after being healed of what everyone thought would surely be a terminal illness. His point was that disease came as the result of sin, and was used by God to make us aware of sin in our life and lead us to repentance. Whether you agree with that is not the issue at this point. What impressed me was the list of sins which followed. "This may be **lack of complete consecration, the assertion of one's own will, confidence in one's strength in performing the Lord's work, a forsaking of the first love and tenderness in the walk with God, or the absence of that gentleness which desires to follow only the leading of the Spirit of God.**"[2]

Far too often, when Christians today think of sin, we think of the obvious, surface-level sins. In one sense, there's nothing wrong with that. Paul does it occasionally in his letters, and a word study of his list in Romans 1, for example, can be quite enlightening. However, the point of the New Covenant is that we have a new relationship with God. It is one of abiding in His presence. It is one in which His laws are written on our hearts (Hebrews 8:10; Jeremiah 31:33). The emphasis here is not that the law is written, but that it is written on our hearts. "The main point in what has been said is this: we have such a high priest, who has taken His seat at the right hand of the throne of the Majesty in the heavens, a minister in the sanctuary, and … the mediator of a better covenant" (Hebrews 8:1-6). "For, on the one hand, there is a setting aside of a former commandment because of its weakness and uselessness (for the Law made nothing perfect), and on the other hand there is a bringing in of a better hope, through which we draw near to God ... so much the more also Jesus has become the guarantee of a better covenant" (Hebrews 7:18-22). "... the word of God, that is the mystery which ... has now been manifested to His saints, ... which is Christ in you the **hope** of glory" (Colossians 1:25-27). The New Covenant relationship with God is one in which the God of heaven Himself, in the person of His Son, takes up residence in the believer, inviting and making the way for the men who were once enemies of God to be made friends with God and to take up residence in the presence of the living God. He administers from heaven the life of heaven to the heart of the believer, so that men who could in no way in their strength please God now, in fact, have the righteousness of God Himself (2 Corinthians 5:14-21). Indeed, since "the way in" is to be in total dependence upon God for the work necessary to accomplish salvation, and since we are to "go on" in the same way that we got in, there can be no more hideous sin than to neglect so great a salvation (Hebrews 2:1-3).

Believer, you may think there is no sin more awful than adultery, homosexuality, divorce, murder, racism, lying, stealing, rape, incest, covetousness, or whatever else there may be that most repulses you. Hear this! For the believer, there is no sin viler than to ignore God's grace and attempt to accomplish His will through some method other than that which He has set forth—total dependence upon and yieldedness to His strength, His ability, administered in your life by His Spirit in the inner man. This dependence characterized your first love and tenderness in your walk with God. In those days, there was a gentleness about you that desired to follow only the Spirit's leading. If Murray's list of sins describes you at any point, please stop now and spend some time in humble repentance. If any of the things we normally think of as sins is a problem in your life, the real problem is sin at the level of intimacy with God. The real problem is lack of faith—unbelief.

> "We rationalize around our sin; we act hypocritically, occasionally we lie and cheat and steal. Then with a shrug, we say 'Well, you know, man, nobody's perfect.' ... Nonsense. When will we start living like those who are free? God says to every one of us, 'Where sin abounded, grace superabounded ... Grace awakens, enlivens, and empowers our ability to conquer sin.
> "Are you ready for a maverick thought? Once we truly grasp the freedom grace brings, we can spend lengthy periods of our lives without sinning or feeling ashamed. Yes, we can. And why not? Why should sin gain the mastery over us? Who says we cannot help but yield to it? How unbiblical. You see, most of us are so programmed to sin that we wait for it to happen.
> "To tell the truth, most Christians have been better trained to expect and handle their sin than to expect and enjoy their freedom."[3]

God calls us to cease from our own labor and enter His rest (Hebrews 4:9). This means we trust Him for our growth, our sanctification, our very life. Jesus declared that man was not made for the Sabbath, but the Sabbath was made for man (Mark 2:27). In doing so, He paved the way for Paul to issue the warning, "Let no one act as your judge in regard to food or drink or in respect to a festival or a new moon or a Sabbath day" (Colossians 2:16). In one sense, this is a declaration of independence from the law. However, neither Paul nor Jesus was proclaiming freedom from the law in any kind of libertarian sense. This is not a license to do anything we want. Rather, it is freedom from approaching life **on the basis of the law.** We answer to a standard higher than that of the scribes and Pharisees, not because we have an even more detailed and specific set of rules to live by, but because our righteousness is Jesus Christ Himself, the One who not only fulfills the law but is the fullness of the Godhead in bodily form. We are called to seek Him, and make knowing Him priority, thereby clothing ourselves with His character.

It is good to read the law. It is good to be familiar with the standard set forth there. God will continue to use it to teach us, to prick our conscience and let us know when we are missing His standard. From it, we can learn of Him and of His character. In it, the scarlet thread of redemption history leads the way to Christ. But if we approach the law as rules to live by and seek to do so in the strength of our determination, even out of a desire to please God, we will find it to be of no use against fleshly indulgence. Only by seeking Christ as our life, can our flesh be reckoned dead in regard to immorality and can we clothe ourselves in Godly character. This is why Paul preached only Christ and Him crucified. There is no other way for the believer to be righteous before God.

Invariably, it seems a discussion of resting in Him and ceasing from our efforts brings up questions. No matter how you answer those questions in the context of discussing rest, people want to shift the discussion to obedience and works: "What of the emphasis in both the Old and New Testaments on obedience? What about 'faith without works is dead?'"

Chapter 5

Dead Faith or Dead Works?

The Role of Obedience

The word "obedience" has always suggested to me, "Here is the rule, now do it." Because of that, although I know God demands obedience, once I began to learn of grace and the concept of "Christ, who **is** my life," I found it difficult to comprehend how "obedience" fits in. If faith without works is dead and works without faith is law, apart from grace and severed from Christ, where is the balance between faith and works?

There are two keys to obedience, and they are found in the words translated "obedience" and "disobedience" in the New Testament. For obedience, one word means, "to allow one's self to be persuaded, yield assent to, obey, or trust." Its counterpart for disobedience means, "unwillingness to be persuaded, willful unbelief that opposes itself to the gracious purpose of God." The emphasis of both these terms has to do with faith, or the lack of it (or, trust and unbelief). So, we see faith is one of the keys to obedience. We will deal with this more later.

The word most often translated simply "to obey" or "obedience," is *hupakouo*. Literally translated, it is "to listen under." It's counterpart, *parakouo*, means "that which has been heard amiss, neglect or refusal to hear," or literally, "to listen alongside." The other key is listening to God.

God used a trip from Ft. Worth to Kansas City, by way of Cleveland, Ohio, to help me understand the concept of obedience a little better.

In September 1981, I was leasing coordinator for a fledgling chain of Christian book stores. Earlier in the company's growth, any time a mall showed an interest in having one of these stores, the company jumped at the chance. They often wound up with a very poor location within the mall. This had happened in Cleveland. Because the mall developers would not negotiate a better location within the mall for our store, the decision was made to send me to close that store and move the product to our Kansas City stores.

With assurances from the president of our company that all the arrangements had been made with the developer, I embarked. I arrived on a Monday afternoon, rented a truck, drove to the mall, and began packing the merchandise in the store into boxes. The mall manager came by and said he had heard nothing of it, and could not permit me to leave until his parent company told him approval had been given for us to leave before the lease expired. He placed a security guard by the door to block my exit. It was too late in the day to call my home office, but I was not particularly concerned at this point because I had a lot of packing to do anyway.

The employees, now out of work, had no incentive to stay beyond their normal hours, so after closing time, the task was mine alone. I finished at about 8:00 the next morning. I called my boss several times during the day to find out what was going on. He first told me he would call the developer and straighten it out, and later told me he had called. He said it was all taken care of with the developer, and the mall manager should get word soon, so I should just load up the truck and go. Shortly after noon, I was able to get the truck loaded, except for one dolly load of boxes, before the mall manager came by and saw what I had done. He had the security guards park their car in front of my truck. At 5:00 P.M., he told me he was going home. He still had no word from his boss, and he could not allow me to leave.

I was furious (not towards the mall manager, but toward the whole situation, and especially towards my boss for lying to me). As I was walking through the mall, I found myself wishing someone would bump into me, or say something rude to me, so I could shove them back. Shocked by the intensity of my anger, I decided to get away from people and walk around the outside of the mall. It was a big mall, which made for a nice, long walk. About halfway around the mall, the Lord broke through my anger and spoke to my heart, "Aren't you supposed to praise me for all things?"

"Lord, I don't feel like praising you right now."

"I didn't ask if you felt like it. I said, 'Aren't you, supposed to?'"

"But Lord, even if I do, I'll just be saying words. It won't be from my heart," I argued.

Patiently, He offered, "Say the words. Praise Me."

Taking a breath, like you would before attempting to tackle a tough, physical task, I said, "Okay. Thank You, Lord, that my boss lied to me. Thank You that I'm stuck here in Cleveland, and my wife is home, pregnant, and could be having a baby anytime now. Thank You that the mall manager put a security guard in front of my truck so I can't leave ...."

As I began this way, the Lord began to soften my heart. The praise became more and more genuine. Within a couple of minutes, I was sincerely giving thanks and singing praise songs and knowing that God was in control of the whole situation.

Then He gave me my solution. Because I was leasing coordinator for the company, I had talked with the leasing agent for the mall developer, had a pretty good relationship with him, and knew the city in which he worked and, hopefully, lived. I went back in the mall, got his number from directory assistance, and called him at home. After I explained the situation to him (no, he had not heard from my boss), he talked to the mall security officers and approved my departure. By 5:30 P.M., I was on my way to Kansas City.

This was a lesson in both praise and obedience. Sometimes it takes a determined effort on our part to embark on the path of obedience. This is repentance. I had to turn from my anger and toward God, much like the prodigal sitting in the pigpen. And like the father who ran to meet his son "while he was still a long way off" and put on him "the best robe," my Father ran to meet me while I was still a long way from heartfelt praise and put on me "the mantle of praise instead of a spirit of fainting."

That day, God spoke to my heart. When that word came, I "listened under." I did not want to praise because I did not see how it would change the situation. Even so, I allowed myself to be persuaded and yielded assent to what He said, trusting that He would not ask anything of me that was not for my good. And I knew, deep inside, He would not allow anything to come against me that was not for my good.

God, in His sovereignty, gave me faith. His word, combined with faith, enabled me to obey. In Hebrews 3:18-4:3, disobedience and unbelief are made synonymous, and faith (belief, and therefore, obedience) combined with the word are proclaimed to be the doorway into His rest. My obedience, however reluctantly it began, was an act of faith. He honored it and gave me rest.

When temptation comes, there is a moment of decision. You may either trust God and yield to Him, or you can trust the tempter and yield to him. Unwilling to be persuaded that God is sufficient to meet your needs, you can refuse to hear what He says about your overwhelming victory through Him who loves you. There is much to be said for a bold, vocal, maybe even shouted, "NO!" in response to temptation. Often that is sufficient to make the world, the flesh, and the devil get in line and leave you alone.

Scripture says, "But He gives a greater grace. Therefore it says, 'God is opposed to the proud, but gives grace to the humble.' Submit, therefore, to God. Resist the devil, and he will flee from you." Experience says, "Hey, I have resisted, and he did not flee. He hung around and kept pestering me and pressing home the temptation, and many times I have eventually given in." Who are you going to listen to? Your experience, or God's word?

We sometimes find ourselves on a parallel course to the will of God. We look like we are heading in the right direction, but we are operating in our strength and ability. This may happen in our efforts to do right, as we discussed when we dealt with Sabbath Rest, or it may occur in our efforts to avoid wrong.

"To listen alongside" does not necessarily head off in the wrong direction. It may look like obedience, heading an exact parallel course to that which has been laid out. However, parallel lines never intersect. If you are on a parallel path, you will not wind up at the same destination.

Obedience "listens *under*." It puts itself under the covering of the gracious will and plan of God, believing that He is faithful. It combines faith with the Word. Place a marble on a table and turn a glass upside down, setting it over the marble. Wherever you move the glass, the marble will go. The believer who walks in the grace whereby he has been saved will go exactly wherever that grace leads him, empowered to go by the very power that moves that grace. Put another way, the believer who, having been saved by the work of Christ on the cross and continues to rest in the finished work of Christ on the cross for his sanctification and growth, will live the Christian life by the enabling power, or ability of God Himself (1 Corinthians 1:18).

The believer who, on the other hand, walks in his strength, striving to please God, obey God, grow himself in the faith, by his ability, falls into legalism, departs from grace, and is rendered powerless, separated from Christ (Galatians 5:4). *His "Christianity" is of no effect, a "non-work." He may be following all the "rules"—reading the Bible, attending church, praying, having a quiet time—looking very Christian, but it's a parallel course. He will never end up where he longs to be, or where God intends him to be—molded in the image of Christ—until all that he does is done in total dependence on God's enabling grace instead of the strength of his human effort.*

Driving along Highway 82 through the rolling hills between Sherman and Gainesville, Texas, as I topped a hill, I could see there were no cars ahead, so I glanced down for just a moment. I heard and felt a rather large thump, followed very quickly by a second one. Looking up, I noticed a wheel cover rolling out across the lane next to me toward the median. My first thought was, "Somebody lost a whole wheel in the road, and I ran over it." However, I immediately noticed a second wheel cover following the first. "Those are my wheel covers! What did I hit?!" Looking in my mirror, I saw a 4" x 4" board lying in the road. My wheel covers rolled over to the shoulder, ran parallel to the car, but quickly began to lose speed until they finally fell over as I was pulling over to go back and get them. I removed the board from the roadway so no one else would hit it, and gathered my wayward wheel covers, so I could put them back where they belonged, on my wheels, *under the wheel wells of my car.*

The lesson is simple. When the wheel covers left my car, they moved off to the side and followed a parallel course. They were headed the same direction my car was, but even if they could have made it to Gainesville, they would not have entered town at the same point my car would. Nor could they have made the turns necessary to reach my ultimate destination south of Fort Worth. The fact is, though, not only would their path cause them to miss the mark, alongside the car, they lacked the power for the journey. They were round and rolled remarkably well. But they had no strength of their own in which to travel. They could only reach the goal attached to the car.

Believer, whenever you take a parallel course, going off to do the work of God in your own strength, or doing religious things that look spiritual but are, in fact, the expression of your own self-interests, you will miss the mark. You will be ineffective and powerless and without direction. However, when you "listen under," when you go on by grace through faith as you got in, when you combine faith with the Word, there is strength and power, the ability of God to do the will of God. There is Rest.

Another message about disobedience is found in Hebrews 3:7-4:8. The word translated disobedience in this passage is *apeitheo*, meaning "unwillingness to be persuaded, willful unbelief that opposes itself *to the gracious purpose of God.*"[1] The writer has just explained that the children of Israel hardened their hearts to the voice of the Lord, and did not believe Him when He told them to enter the Land. Yet, he is quoting from the book of Psalms, written long after the Israelites had entered the promised land. In chapter three, he emphasizes the warning, "Today if you hear His voice, do not harden your hearts …," is still valid for us today. In chapter four, he makes the application that the Sabbath Rest is also still remaining for us today.

He makes the transition from one chapter to the next with these words:

> "And to whom did He swear that they should not enter His rest, but to those who were disobedient? And so we see that they were not able to enter because of unbelief. Therefore, let us fear lest, while a promise remains of entering His rest, anyone of you should seem to have come short of it. For indeed we have had good news preached to us, just as they also; but the word they heard did not profit them, because it was not united by faith in those who heard. For we who have believed enter that rest."
> Hebrews 3:18-4:3a

Disobedience (*apeitheo*) in verse 18 is paralleled and equated with unbelief (*apisteuo*—"not faithing," willful unbelief) in verse 19. It is a cause for fear. Look at the end of Hebrews 4:1, "... if anyone of you may seem to have **come short of it.**" This is one of two places in scripture where this expression is used. The other is Romans 3:23, "All have sinned and **come short of** the glory of God." Elsewhere, the word is translated "to be behind," "to come after," "to lack," "to be in want," "suffer need." We *need* the glory of God. We *need* His sabbath rest. Sin causes you to come short of the glory of God. It also causes you to come short of His rest. Lack of faith, or refusal to have faith (to trust, to believe), holds us back, so that we follow behind (not under). Again, as with *parakouo* (disobedience that listens "alongside"), here, *apeitheo*, disobedience holds us back, and equated with *apisteuo* (unbelief), causes us to come up behind, falling short. You may even still be heading in the right direction, but like Moses and his generation of Israelites, you never seem to reach the promised land.

In these last days, God has spoken to us in His Son. This Word is greater than the word spoken through the prophets and the angels to the patriarchs of the old covenant. This Word, Himself, is greater than the angels (Hebrews 1:5-14). He is greater than Moses (Hebrews 3:1-6). He is greater than Aaron (the Levitical priesthood) (Hebrews 7:1-10). He is the outward expression of the invisible God, the radiance (or outshining) of His glory (Hebrews 1:3). We must give more abundant heed to this Word that has been spoken to us. He is worthy of our attention. He is worthy of our confidence. He **is** a rewarder of those that diligently seek Him. If we truly believe that, it **will** cause us to seek Him diligently. We **will** give more abundant heed. We will combine this Word with faith in our hearts. The word the fathers received did not profit them because it was not united by faith in those who heard. We who have believed do enter that rest. The Word which we have heard is the living Word, the Son of God, and the only Way to the Father in Heaven. To doubt this, even in the least, is to call God a liar. To doubt it, even the tiniest degree is heinous sin, and it will cause us to come short of all He offers us. To fully accept this is our path to the abiding presence of God and Sabbath Rest.

If you are struggling with sin or temptation, you are not resting. You are struggling. Choose rest. It is at the end of his great passage on rest that the writer of Hebrews declares:

> *And there is no creature hidden from His sight,*
> *but all things are open and laid bare to the eyes of Him*
> *with whom we have to do. Therefore, since we have*
> *a great high priest who has passed through the heavens,*
> *Jesus the Son of God, let us hold fast our confession.*
> *For we do not have a high priest who cannot sympathize*
> *with our weaknesses, but one who has been tempted*
> *in all things as we are, yet without sin. Therefore let*
> *us draw near with confidence to the throne of grace, so that*
> *we may receive mercy and find grace to help in time of need.*
> Hebrews :13-16

EXTREME *Gratitude*

There is nothing to hide from Him. He sees your sin, your temptation, and your weakness. And to give you confidence to come before Him, He put on the throne His own Son, who was one of us. He lived here and faced everything you face, yet without sin. Now He is on the throne of heaven, ministering the life of heaven to all who draw near.

This is rest. When temptation comes, you identify and choose to avoid it. You then, by your actions, more than by your words, draw near to God. You submit to God and rest in the victory of Jesus Christ on your behalf over even the temptation. If Satan persists with accusations or tempting, you can simply say, "If I struggle with you, I am not resting. I choose rest." You do not simply resist the devil. Nor do you submit to God, step one, and resist the devil, step two. Rather, you resist the devil by humbly yielding to God's grace, administered by your sinless high priest from the throne of grace, and the devil will flee.

Obedience, however, is not just "not disobeying." Obedience is also hearing what God says and doing it. One problem we face as Christians is being caught between two extremes. One says, "Jesus is in me, so I am just going to sit here and do nothing until He does it through me." The other says, "God says to do this, and I am going to get out there and work, work, work until I get it done." A third pattern seeks to strike a balance, saying, "Do all you can do and leave the rest to God." Even this falls short of the New Testament pattern: "Christ is all and in all." The question comes, "How? I fail so easily. Where is the power to be a doer and not a hearer only?"

John 15 records Jesus' teaching about the vine and the branches:

> *I Am the vine, and My Father is the vinedresser.*
> *Every branch in Me that does not bear fruit, He takes*
> *away; and every branch that bears fruit, He prunes it,*
> *so that it may bear more fruit. You are already clean because*
> *of the word which I have spoken to you. Abide in Me,*

and I in you. As the branch cannot bear fruit of itself unless it abides in the vine, so neither can you, unless you abide in Me. I am the vine, you are the branches; he who abides in Me, and I in him, he bears much fruit; for apart from Me you can do nothing.

John 15:1-5

Jesus is the vine. The vine is the woody stalk through which the sap (the life of the vine) flows, carrying nutrients to the branches to produce fruit. As the branch grows, it also is woody and looks like the vine. However, the longer the branch grows, the more the life-giving efforts of the vine go to sustaining the branch, and the less sap goes to producing fruit. This is why "every branch that bears fruit, He prunes it, that it may bear more fruit." A grapevine branch is pruned back to the basal bud, the bud closest to the base of the branch. This does not leave much branch but allows more of the sap to go into the production of fruit. You see, it is not the responsibility of the branch to produce fruit. It is the responsibility of the vine to produce fruit. The branch only bears it.

We do not prove we are followers of Jesus (disciples) by looking like Jesus. We can do all kinds of "spiritual" and religious deeds, and look to all the world like very religious people. Some will look at us and think this is what Jesus looks like. But they are just seeing an overgrown stalk of wood with maybe a little undernourished fruit scattered along the course of its life.

Jesus said, "By this is My Father glorified, that you bear fruit, and so prove to be My disciples." It takes only a very small branch to bear fruit. To the degree the life of the vine (the Spirit of God) does not have to sustain the life of a long, woody branch is the degree the fruit of the Spirit can be produced in our lives. It will be full, luscious fruit that will satiate the hunger and quench the thirst of a dying world.

Now, what do you want to be? A long stalk of wood that looks like the vine? Or would you rather decrease that He may

EXTREME Gratitude

increase? Do you want people to look at you and see you trying to look like Jesus, but failing and fruitless? Or do you want them to see the luscious fruit that bursts forth from a life abiding in the Vine?

Chapter 6

Extreme Righteousness

Outdoing the Pharisees

"The Ten Commandments are not ten suggestions." I have no idea who originated that quote, but I have heard it most of my life. We are told, and have sung that we are to "trust and obey for there's no other way." Jesus said, "If you love me, you will keep my commandments" (John 14:15), and "If you keep My commandments, you will abide in My love ... You are My friends if you do what I command you" (John 15:10, 14).

Then, there is the "biggie"—the clincher, the one that proves without a doubt that we are still obligated to obey all the Law, all the rules of the Bible—Old Testament and New:

> "Do not think that I come to abolish the Law or the Prophets; I did not come to abolish them but to fulfill. For truly, I say to you, until heaven and earth pass away, not the smallest letter or stroke[1] shall pass from the Law until all is accomplished."
> Matthew 5:17-18

How can you argue with that? You cannot.

What does it mean to fulfill? What does it mean to accomplish? What was the focus of the Law and the Prophets? Was it to establish rules to live by? Or, was it to point to Christ?

According to Paul, in Galatians 3, the Law was a tutor or schoolmaster, to bring us to Christ. Paul says we were "kept in custody under the law, being shut up to the faith that was later to be revealed." It has been revealed. That was accomplished so that we are no longer under a tutor, but are justified by faith, not by law.

We are called to a righteousness that exceeds that of the Pharisees. This is not just a higher standard of rules for behavior.

It's a higher righteousness that comes from God on the basis of faith and has an effect on our relationships with both God and man.

What was the purpose of the feast days and observances? They all, in one way or another, were designed to symbolize the provision of God, the coming of Christ, and to cause God's people to pay attention to God and keep their focus on Him. Under the New Covenant, all have been set aside. Jesus is the bread of life. He feeds us. We have baptism to symbolize our initial immersion into the faith, through His death, burial and resurrection becoming our own. We have the Lord's Supper to symbolize our daily dying to self and going on in the faith. It's all about Him, and in Him, the feasts were all fulfilled.

What was the purpose of circumcision? It showed ownership, in effect. It showed that the individual belonged to and obeyed God. It set the Hebrew men apart from the rest of the world. Jesus sent His Holy Spirit to indwell His people. He lives within us to empower us, to enable us to live for God, according to His will. It is His indwelling presence and the lifestyle that He produces in us that sets us apart. It is the love we have for one another that demonstrates to the world that He exists, and we belong to Him.

Furthermore, He took wounds in His flesh and shed His blood for our redemption and righteousness. Circumcision is no longer needed to set us apart or to demonstrate that we are His people. We have His indwelling presence in the person of the Holy Spirit—His fulfilled promise and the pledge (or earnest) of our inheritance.

What was the tithe and its purpose? Primarily it was food—meat, grain, and wine—which was brought and dedicated to God to seek atonement for sins. It was brought out of the harvest and culled from the livestock according to specific guidelines for specific feasts. It was then consumed in a great feast, a party. What remained was given to the priests , who had food to eat because they did not own or cultivate land of their own. Since we don't have the same kind of priesthood today, is it needed? No, and yes. If you are part of a church that has buildings, and bills to pay, and a hierarchical clergy/laity style leadership, then, yes. They need you to help pay the bills. Does that have to be a tithe (10%)? No. The New Covenant model is that **everything** you have belongs to God. Not 10%, but 100%. Give enough to the local church of which you are a part to help it meet its financial obligations. The rest (all of it, 100%) you should use wisely and as a good steward, seeking God's guidance for how you should use it. You should work diligently to earn enough for you and your family to have food, clothing, and shelter, and enough extra to help others who are in need. Whatever the Lord leads you to give to your church is enough—10%, more, or less. However, a tithe for God is **not** enough. Righteousness that exceeds that of the Pharisees yields everything to God's control and follows His leadership in the stewardship of it.

A righteousness that exceeds that of the Pharisees isn't just don't murder. It also involves not being angry or judgmental or condescending. It isn't just don't commit adultery. It is don't lust after another person. It isn't just don't make false vows. It is don't make any vows to prove your veracity, but simply answer with an honest yes or no. It isn't an eye for an eye and a tooth for a tooth. It is go the second mile to help someone, even if their initial intent was to take advantage of you. It isn't just "love your neighbor and hate your enemy." It is "love your enemy, too, and pray for them."

Don't do religious things like give to the poor, pray, or fast in order to show your religion. Do them. Just do them in humility and faithfulness to God. Quit smacking people in the head with the two-by-four in your eye while saying you're trying to get the sawdust out of theirs. If you know how you want to be treated, then you know how you want to be loved. Love other people the same way.

The law has not been done away with. Jesus did not destroy the Law. He brought it into all its fullness in Himself. It was not done away with, but rather, it came to be. Jesus declared it so when upon the cross, He cried out, "It is finished," and with the tearing of His body, the veil was torn between God and man so that we may enter into the Holy of Holies and there abide in the presence of the living God. This takes it beyond rules and regulations. It strikes at the very core of religion itself.

What was the purpose of the Old Testament priesthood? It provided a mediator between God and man. It provided someone whose life was dedicated to the Lord, if at times in ceremony only, who was permitted to offer sacrifices on behalf of the rest of the people. Jesus came as a priest after the order of Melchizedek—meaning he had no recorded beginning or end but was eternal. Jesus' priesthood was not based on the law, but on the power of an eternal, indestructible life. In addition, Jesus was descended from the tribe of Judah by His earthly lineage. This was not the priestly tribe. So, the priesthood changed. The old law was put away as weak and useless. Jesus fulfilled its purpose with an eternal priesthood.

What was the purpose of the Old Testament sacrificial system? It provided atonement, one day a year, and through repeated sacrifices, daily, weekly, monthly, annually. More than that, it pointed to Jesus. As we observed in chapter 2, regarding atonement, the whole temple and sacrificial system had symbolism that pointed to God's eternal provision for the sins of men. His blood was more effective than that of bulls and goats, and His was a once for all sacrifice. Those sacrifices could not make the worshiper perfect (whole, clean, complete) in conscience. But His sacrifice is able to cleanse your conscience from dead works to serve the living God. He fulfilled the purpose of the sacrificial system.

What was the purpose of the Sabbath? It was to remind people to focus on God by having a day of rest. It was to remind them to rest from their labors as God "rested" on the seventh day of creation. Jesus came as Lord of the Sabbath and declared that it was made for man, not the other way around. He established a relationship with God based solely on faith, both for salvation and sanctification. He fulfilled the purpose of the Sabbath by opening a way for man to rest in Him 24 hours a day, seven days a week. The Sabbath is not one day a week. Nor is it one or two or five or ten hours spread over one or two or three days a week.

What was the purpose of the tabernacle and temple? It provided a place for God to dwell among and interact with His people. His indwelling was symbolized by His filling the tabernacle and later the temple with fire and smoke when they were dedicated. His ongoing presence was symbolized by the "*showbread*." When the disciples were gathered in Jerusalem, the Holy Spirit came into the room. But the place was not filled with fire and smoke. A flame came and lit upon each one of them, showing that each believer, not the building, is the dwelling place of God. Each believer is filled with the Holy Spirit. And the living Bread of life abides within them to show that they are His. He fulfilled the symbolism of the temple by choosing to indwell His people—the great mystery of the ages—Christ in you, the hope of glory.

David declared in Psalm 84: "How lovely are Your dwelling places, O Lord of Hosts! My soul longed and even yearned for the courts of the Lord; My heart and my flesh sing for joy to the living God. For a day in Your courts is better than a thousand ...." As a child, in Sunday School, I remember singing Psalm 122:1, "I was glad when they said unto me, let us go into the house of the Lord."

When I read Andrew Murray's *The Holiest of All*, I saw as never before that God really had made a way for me to be His dwelling place, and for me to abide forever in His Presence, beginning in this lifetime, not just after I die. If I thought I was glad to "go into the house of the Lord," I was awed and overjoyed to be the house of the Lord (Hebrews 3:6). Since then, I have begun to realize more and more of the implications of this truth.

This goes way beyond being "the 'temple of the Holy Spirit' so do not sin but 'flee immorality'" (1 Corinthians 6:12-20). God knew that you would sin. He knew that when He saved you, it was only the beginning. He knew that there would be times when you would fail and dishonor Him. He loved you and chose to save you and lavish His grace on you anyway (Ephesians 1:7, 8). More than that, He chose **you** to be His dwelling place. He chose to meet with you in person, day-by-day, by making His Son the Mercy Seat and making your heart His home. He put the meeting place between God and man **in you! In your innermost being**! He did this even knowing beforehand what struggles you would face as you grow in your relationship with Him. He knew everything you would do, and everything that would be done to you, and chose you anyway.

We love Him because He first loved us. God is the prime mover. He put in place His plan of redemption before the foundation of the world—a once and for all way to ensure that we could abide in His presence. That relentless, lavish grace calls to our hearts to serve and follow Him. When we see it and accept it, it overwhelms us and elicits a response of love that longs to be as passionate as His love for us.

I have heard and sung a number of praise songs based on Psalm 84. As I sang, "How lovely your dwelling place, how precious it is to me," or "I love to live in Your house, O Lord," or "How lovely is Thy dwelling place," I knew the New Covenant concept that I am His house. Still, singing this Psalm, I knew David probably wrote it with the tabernacle in mind, and his own desire to build a temple for the Lord. I knew most Christians, probably including those who wrote and recorded these praise songs based on this Psalm, were thinking of Christians gathering inside the church building. So, for many years, knowing that He chose on Pentecost to indwell His people instead of a building, I would sing these songs and "translate" them in my mind to something like, "how lovely is the concept of being God's dwelling place."

Finally, I have realized it is more than a concept. I am His dwelling place, and, to Him, I am lovely! Let that grab you! You are His dwelling place, by His doing, by His choice. You are lovely, by His doing! He has made you lovely. He has qualified you to share in the inheritance of the saints in light! (Colossians 1:12). He has blessed you with every spiritual blessing in the heavens in Christ Jesus (Ephesians 1:3). You are beautiful. He makes you beautiful. He makes you lovely. He dwells in you. It is His choice. He who began a good work in you will perfect it until the day of Christ Jesus (Philippians 1:6). You are loved by God, and as my friend, Jack Taylor, put it, "There is nothing you can do about it."

The King James Version says, "How amiable are thy tabernacles." Webster's dictionary defines amiable as "having a pleasant and friendly disposition; good-natured." It further defines it as "lovely or lovable," in other words, having qualities that make one likable. However, the Hebrew word used here comes from a root word meaning "to boil," and is used as a way of saying "to love." Wow, a boiling, hot, churning love is an amazing description of God's love for you, His dwelling place.

I don't just love the concept of being His house; I love being His house! I love being loved by and lived in by Him. I am free! I am free to love Him. I am free to praise Him. I am free to worship Him. I am free to faith Him. I am free to thank Him. I am free to live for Him. Whatever He calls me to do, He gives me the ability to do it by His indwelling presence and power. It is God who is at work in you both to will and to work for His good pleasure. He is writing His word on your heart and making it a part of your core being, your spiritual and mental DNA, so that you can walk in His will, pleasing Him in all things.

This is extreme righteousness. This is extreme Christianity, or dare I say, Christian extremism. It is not about following the law to the extreme. It is not about forcing Christianity on others or fiercely defending it, especially in any physical sense. Extremism for the follower of Christ is following Him. Extremism for the Christian is making knowing Him our top priority, and then allowing Him to live through us, to enable us by His doing and

His power and His wisdom, righteousness, sanctification, and redemption to be holy and blameless and innocent, abiding now and through eternity in the presence of our living, Holy God and enjoying fellowship with Him.

Chapter 7

Little Faith

James 2:17 says, "Even so faith, if it has no works, is dead, being by itself." The message of the New Covenant is that His law is written on our hearts. He is at work to will (desire) and to work (do). You are saved by grace through faith, and that is not of yourselves, it is the gift of God, not of works, lest any man should boast. And the way you get in is the way you go on.

Lest we do nothing and blame it on God's failure to motivate or activate us, James comes in with a strong challenge. Faith works. If you believe God is sufficient, it will affect your actions. If you believe He loves you, that He is a person, that He desires fellowship with you, you will not seek to fill the void in your life with anything else. Let me restate that. If you are falling prey to any sin, particularly any habitual, ensnaring sin, then you do not believe God is who He says He is or loves you the way He says He does or is sufficient to fill the emptiness in your heart.

It was "by faith Abraham when he was called, obeyed by going out to a place which he was to receive for an inheritance; and he went out not knowing where he was going. By faith he lived as an alien in the land of promise, as in a foreign land, dwelling in tents with Isaac and Jacob, fellow heirs of the same promise; for he was looking for the city which has foundations, whose architect and builder is God" (Hebrews 11:8-10). Abraham heard the call of God. He believed (it is unfortunate that we do not have a verb form of the word "faith" in English) God's promise. The only response that faith allowed was to go where God said. To not go would be to say that God was not faithful to His word. But notice where his focus was. He did not go looking for an earthly city, but one whose architect and builder was God. He did not know where he was going, but He knew that God was able to supply him whatever He promised. His faith was expressed through obedience.

The next verse (Hebrews 11:11) says: "By faith, even Sarah herself received the ability to conceive, even beyond the proper time of life, since she considered Him faithful who had promised." Wow! What an example. He who promised is faithful. Sarah "faithed" this fact. She had no ability to do what God had said. She was not able to bear a child. God promised she and her "as good as dead" husband would be parents. By her faith, she "received ability."

You see, the way you get in is the way you go on. The faith that saved you was not of your own doing; it was the gift of God so that even in your faith, you could not boast any part in the act of salvation. The way you get in is the way you go on. The faith to do the will of God is not of your own doing. It is the gift of God, so you will not boast in what wonderful things you have done for God in your life. In that faith comes the divine "*dunamis*," the ability, the power, to do the will of God, because He that promised is faithful. He is at work both to will and to work for His good pleasure.

If you truly have faith, you will act on it. He will enable you to. If you do not choose to do His will, it is because you lack faith. If you do not choose to resist temptation, it is because you lack faith. If you are "unable" to do what He has said, it is because you lack faith. If you say you have faith, and you do not have the works to go along with it, then your faith is at best "little faith."

There have been times I thought that if I lived in the days where men were identified by their first name and the city of their residence, I would have been known as "Ohyee of Littlefaith." God has often surprised me with His faithfulness in ways that have gently confronted me with my shortage of faith in a given situation.

Jesus refers to his disciples as men of little faith on five occasions. Each time, He gives a different explanation for their condition. The first is found in the sermon on the mount in Matt. 6:30-31: "But if God so clothes the grass of the field, which is alive today and tomorrow is thrown into the furnace, will He not much more clothe you, O men of little faith? Do not worry then ...."

There is no need for worry or anxiety because "He cares for you" (1 Peter 5:7). Jesus says that if you will make seeking His kingdom and His righteousness your top priority, Your Father will provide everything you have need of. Don't be anxious about tomorrow either. You do not have grace for tomorrow. You have grace for each day as it comes, and each event of each day, as you need it, and not before (Matthew 6:33-34). You must trust that He is sovereign and will allow nothing to happen to you that He is unable to use to mold you into the image of Christ. If this is true, then no situation is worth being worried or upset over. Anxiety is a faith inhibitor.

Jesus' second teaching on little faith is found in Matthew 8:24-26: "And behold, there arose a great storm on the sea, so that the boat was being covered with the waves; but Jesus Himself was asleep. And they came to Him and woke Him, saying, 'Save us, Lord; we are perishing!' And He said to them, 'Why are you afraid [cowardly, timid, esp. the inward sensation of fear], you men of little faith?' Then He got up and rebuked the winds and the sea, and it became perfectly calm."

It has been said that fear is faith in the negative; that it is the belief that bad is going to happen, and there is no hope for good; it is the opposite of faith. It may not be a direct opposite. It is a faith inhibitor—both a cause and a result of lack of faith. The disciples saw the storm as a harbinger of death. Jesus saw only life. He was not afraid of the storm. He knew He had power over it, so He told it to be calm, and it obeyed Him. When the storms of life blow, you can know the calm and peace you long for if you truly believe that God is concerned for your wellbeing and that He has power over the storms. You must believe that He is God and that He will reward you if you will put Him first (Hebrews 11:6).

The third inhibitor of faith is doubt. In Matthew 14:28-31: "Peter said to Him, 'Lord, if it is You, command me to come to

You on the water.' And He said, 'Come!' And Peter got out of the boat and walked on the water and came toward Jesus. But seeing the wind, he became frightened, and beginning to sink, he cried out, 'Lord, save me!' Immediately Jesus stretched out His hand and took hold of him, and said to him, 'You of little faith, why did you doubt?'"

Faith walks on water. Doubt sinks. Faith looks on Him. Doubt looks at the storms. But even when you find yourself sinking, look once again to Him, and He will lift you up.

In Matthew 16:6-11a: "And Jesus said to them, 'Watch out and beware of the leaven of the Pharisees and Sadducees.' They began to discuss this among themselves, saying, 'He said that because we did not bring any bread.' But Jesus, aware of this, said, 'You men of little faith. Why do you discuss among yourselves that you have no bread? Do you not yet understand or remember the five loaves of the five thousand, and how many baskets full you took up? Or the seven loaves of the four thousand, and how many large baskets full you took up? How is it that you do not understand that I did not speak to you concerning bread?'"

In this example, it is a lack of understanding and a failure to remember, which prompts the description, "you men of little faith." What has God done for you? Did He not take on flesh and blood that He might render of no effect the work of Satan in the world? What Satan did to separate men from God by sin, Jesus undid to reconcile you to God by His righteousness, by His torn flesh that opened the veil into the holy of holies, and by His shed blood that cleanses away your sins. Is it not true that "He who began a good work in you will perfect it"? (Philippians 1:6). Do you not understand that "He who did not spare His own Son, but delivered Him over for us all, how will He not also with Him freely give us all things?" (Romans 8:32).

Finally, in Matthew 17:14-20, Jesus descends from the Mount of Transfiguration to find his disciples unable to help a man who had come seeking healing for his son. His initial response is, "O unbelieving and perverted generation, how long shall I be with you? How long shall I put up with you?" After Jesus cast the demon out of the boy and healed him, "Then the disciples came to Jesus privately and said, 'Why could we not cast it out?' And He said to them, 'Because of the littleness of your faith; for truly I say to you, if you have faith as a mustard seed, you shall say to this mountain, "Move from here to there," and it shall move; and nothing shall be impossible to you.'"

How small is little faith? Jesus says all we need is faith as a mustard seed. Could "little faith" be smaller even than a mustard seed? What is faith like a mustard seed?

Two of Abraham's acts in Genesis 12-22 are included in the "Roll Call of Faith" in Hebrews 11. The first we have looked at—his willingness to leave his home and go to a land, which God would show him, not knowing where he was going. The other was his response to God's testing him when he was ready to sacrifice Isaac as a burnt offering. Most of us would concur that both of these events are examples of faith, and somewhat extreme examples at that.

What would it take for you to follow either of these examples? What would it take for you to pack up all your belongings and move your family to a new location, not knowing ahead of time where exactly you were going, just knowing that God would tell you when you got there?

I looked up faith in a thesaurus and found four definitions:

1. A system of religious belief.
2. Absolute certainty in the trustworthiness of another.
3. Mental acceptance of the truth or actuality of something.
4. Those who accept and practice a particular religious belief.

If God told you to take your child and offer him as a burnt offering, would your system of religious beliefs give you sufficient courage to do it? Would mental acceptance of the truth that God said it be enough to make you take your child and kill him or her? Would being part of a group of people who share your religious beliefs enable you to do such a thing?

If I could change any one thing about the English language, it would be the fact that "faith" is not a verb. We have the noun "faith." When we try to describe that concept as an action, we have to say "have faith." Instead, we usually use "believe" or "trust." I think we lose, or ignore, some of the impact of the meaning of "faith." Perhaps that is why we have definitions for the word faith like, "A system of religious beliefs, or those who practice those beliefs," and "mental acceptance of the truth of something." These definitions do not require significant action. These definitions allow us to stay within the safe zone of things we can understand with our minds.

To do what Abraham did would take nothing less than absolute dependence on the trustworthiness (faithfulness, reliability, dependability) of God. Not just accepting this as true, but a willingness to act on that truth, knowing that the course of action you are taking will end in absolute disaster if that truth is not true.

In other words, if God is not being honest with you, if in any measure He is not trustworthy, you or someone around you will face death, or at the very best, significant suffering. Faith, as "absolute certainty of the trustworthiness of another," on the other hand, may cause us to let go of everything that we know by education or personal experience, and act solely on the basis of what this "Another" says.

Let's take a closer look at mustard seed faith, using Abraham's faith to illustrate it. One of the first things we will see is that mustard seed faith does not eliminate the possibility of failure.

Genesis 12:1-3: God's promise was given, and Abraham was told to go to a new land that God would show him, and there God would make of him a great nation and would bless him. He was already 75 years old, and in an act of faith, Abraham went to the land. Yet, a few verses later in Genesis 12, when famine came, he did not wait for "the blessing," but went to Egypt. Then, fearing the Egyptians might kill him in order to get his wife, he told them Sarah was his sister. God had to intervene. "The Lord struck Pharaoh and his house with great plagues because of Sarai, Abram's wife" (vs. 17). He had promised to make Abraham a great nation, and He did not want the mother of that nation defiled by the pharaoh. In addition, this may well be when they acquired Hagar, Sarah's Egyptian maid, which set them up for their next failure.

Genesis 15:6: Eleven years have passed since God's promise was first given. He had no children, and assumed one of his slaves would be his heir. But now God promised him a son from his own body, and descendants that would outnumber the stars. "Abraham believed God, and it was credited to him as righteousness" (Romans 4:3). Yet, a short time later, he yielded to Sarah's pressure and had a child by her handmaiden, Hagar. Abraham was then 86 years old.

Each time God appeared to Abraham, He told him a little more about His plans. Genesis 17:1-8: When Abraham was 99, God appeared to him again and told him once again that he would have a son, and many descendants, and one seed through whom all the world would be blessed. He assured him specifically that Sarah would be the mother of the promised son, and that the child would be born within 12 months. Yet, in the three months that followed, Abraham once again passed Sarah off as his sister instead of his wife, in order to save his hide. Again, God intervened, appearing to Abimilech in a dream and warning him he was dead if he proceeded with his plans to take Sarah as his wife.

Are these the acts of a man of faith? How could God make of him a great nation, bless him, bless the whole world through his descendants, and specifically through his wife Sarah, if Abraham was dead? God's promise meant that Abraham would not die, at least until the child was born. He had nothing to fear. He was invulnerable. But he did fear. As a result, he lied, he deceived others, he tried to make God's plan happen in his strength by having a child through his wife's maid and even risked his wife's purity. And most of this after "He believed in the Lord and He reckoned it to him as righteousness" (Genesis 15:6).

His faith at this point did not prevent his failures. However, we will see that mustard seed faith is not negated by failure.

The fact is, if you look in the Old Testament at the lives of many of the heroes, you find a variety of sins and failures: Noah, Abraham, Isaac, Jacob, Judah, Moses, David, Solomon. Yet when treated by the New Testament, you find none of their failures. The grace of God presents them as examples of faith and reveals the good things for which we honor and admire them to this day.

In Romans 4, Abraham is presented as the spiritual ancestor of all those who live by faith. It is said of him that though he was old, and he and Sarah were both physically dead to the possibility of having children, he believed God, "who gives life to the dead." Even as he considered their physical condition, which is described "as good as dead since he was about 100 years old," it is said he did so "without becoming weak in faith." Romans 4:19 sums it up, "He did not waver in unbelief, but grew strong in faith, giving glory to God, and being fully assured that what God had promised, He was able to perform."

Is this a discrepancy in Scripture? Does the Word of God contradict itself? Never. There is great comfort here for you and me. Abraham believed God from the start. It was faith that enabled him to leave his home and travel to a land that God would show him. When the word came, promising to make him a great nation, he "faithed" God, and it was put down in his spiritual account book as righteousness. According to Scripture, even as the years passed, and he considered his and Sarah's age, he did not waver in his faith. However, during this time, he did grow strong in faith, giving glory to God.

Mustard seed faith does not necessarily prevent failure. Nor is it negated by failure. The key is this, like any living thing, mustard seed faith is characterized by growth. When Jesus compared the kingdom of heaven to a mustard seed, His emphasis was on its growth: it starts small, but when it is full-grown, it is a tree in which birds can make their nests. If Abraham's faith had been the same at the beginning as it was in the end, there would have been no growth. If his faith had been the same when the promise was given as it was when the promise was fulfilled, there would likely have been no failures along the way. The failures and sins did not negate the faith. It is the testimony of God's Word that he did not waver in unbelief. He did not become weak in faith. However, he was not perfect. There was room for growth, and he did grow in faith.

As I look back on my life, I can see a string of sin and failure—many things I regret were ever a part of my history. I find great hope that when I stand before God and He looks back on my life, He will see the faith I began with and the faith I end with, and His testimony will be "you did not become weak, you did not waver in unbelief, but you did grow," and when all is said and done, He will say, "well done."

How can we grow from where we are to where we need to be? Like any seed, mustard seed faith must die in order to live.

Genesis chapters 1-11 tell of the fall & corruption of mankind, through which man lost the life of paradise, and death entered the world. In Genesis 12:3, the promise to Abraham was that in him, all the families of the earth shall be blessed. In Galatians 3:16, we read: "Now the promises were spoken to Abraham and his seed. He does not say, 'and to seeds,' as referring to many, but rather to one, 'and to your seed,' that is Christ." Jesus was the fulfillment of the promise to bless "all the families of the earth" in Abraham. The promise of a child to Abraham and Sarah went beyond the birth of Isaac. It was the beginning of the ancestry of the savior. Abraham was to become the father of the One who was before him. The man, "now good as dead," became the path God chose to bring life back to mankind. Through him, God established the pattern: Life always comes out of death.

In Hebrews 11, both Sarah and Abraham appear in the roll call of faith. "By faith, even Sarah herself received the ability to conceive even beyond the proper time of life, since she considered

Him faithful who had promised." Genesis 21:1-2 describes it this way: "Then the Lord took note of Sarah as He had said, and the Lord did for Sarah as He had promised. So Sarah conceived and bore a son to Abraham in his old age, at the appointed time of which God had spoken to him." She considered Him faithful who had promised. And the Lord did for Sarah as He had promised. Sarah trusted His promise because she rested in the truth that God Himself is faithful. He is trustworthy. As a result, she received the ability to conceive. This was not something she and Abraham engineered. She received it. New life must come from God. It is not something we manufacture by our efforts or earn by our goodness. In Isaac, God proved himself to be the giver of life. The new nation God had promised came by God's doing, born from one "as good as dead."

If you have work to do that you are unable to do, you can turn to someone who is trained to do it. If you are building a house, perhaps you can do most of the carpentry work, but need an electrician to do the wiring, or a plumber to run the pipes and prepare the water and drainage lines. Or, perhaps some work needs to be done on your car that is beyond your ability. You go to a trained mechanic, someone with more training and experience than yourself. You have a barber to cut your hair, a dentist to care for your teeth, a doctor to discern your medical needs and treatment, and, hopefully, a professional photographer to create your portrait. Every day we recognize our limitations and lay aside our desire to do for ourselves, and we "faith" those whose capabilities exceed our own. We trust that if they begin the task, they will complete it skillfully and correctly. If we refuse to die to our desires and accept our inadequacy for the task, we often suffer the consequences of our pride, with flying sparks, leaky pipes, or extra parts for our still unrepaired auto. Few of these professionals are truly primarily concerned for our wellbeing in the completion of their work. Yet we trust them. Does it not make even more sense to lay aside our efforts to perfect ourselves spiritually and put out faith in the One who created us and saved us, to complete us as well? Is it not a reasonable faith to trust in the One who loved us enough to die for us, to complete that which He began in us, and do it right, and do it to our benefit?

Hebrews 11:6 says, "and without faith, it is impossible to please Him, for He who comes to God must believe that He is and that He is a rewarder of those who seek Him." Jeremiah 29:11-13 reads: "'For I know the plans I have for you,' says the Lord, 'Plans for welfare and not for calamity, to give you a future and a hope. Then you will call upon Me and come and pray to Me, and I will listen to you. You will seek Me and find Me when you search for Me with all your heart.'" It is necessary to believe, not only that God exists, but that when you seek Him out, He will be found. When you ask Him for life, He has provided it through Christ and will make it available to you. When you need strength for daily living, He will be that strength for you. When you need patience, He will give it. When you need steadfastness in your Christian walk, He has made a way. When you need love for someone you find difficulty loving, He is love and will make love alive inside you. We must die to our desires, and accept our inadequacy for the task and turn to the One who made us, and desires to complete us.

It took 25 years from the time he first received the promise from God until the birth of Isaac, and Abraham wasn't exactly the ideal model of patiently waiting. Perhaps his failures played a significant part in his learning that God is faithful. He and Sarah could not accomplish it on their own; it had to be from God. None of their solutions worked—it was not through the slave, Eliezer, or the handmaid, Hagar. When in fear, he lied and risked Sarah's purity to protect his own life, God intervened to protect Sarah from being defiled, so that the promise could be fulfilled by His doing.

Abraham learned the lesson. "By faith Abraham, when he was tested, offered up Isaac ... He considered that God is able to raise people even from the dead ..." (Hebrews 11:17-19). Having finally received the promise, he was tested. However, he had learned that life comes from God, and God brings life out of death. Only absolute certainty in the trustworthiness of God could bring Abraham to the point of laying his promised son on an altar and taking his life. His faith had grown to the level of knowing that since God had promised that through Isaac God would give Abraham more descendants than the sand on the seashore or stars in the sky, if Isaac died, even if God said "Kill Isaac," God would raise Isaac from the dead and still fulfill his promise to Abraham. In a sense, or in parable form, according to the writer of Hebrews, Abraham received Isaac back from the dead, and God's promise to make him a great nation was fulfilled through Isaac.

You see, we are "always carrying about in the body the dying of Jesus, so that the life of Jesus also may be manifested in our body" (2 Corinthians 4:10). Jesus said, "If anyone wishes to come after Me, he must him deny himself, take up his cross daily, and follow Me" (Luke 9:23). "Unless a grain of wheat falls into the earth and dies, it remains alone, but if dies, it bears much fruit" (John 12:24).

Jesus's question, "How long shall I be with you?" may well have come from His awareness that His time on earth was drawing to an end, and the faith of His disciples was still little, with no signs of growth. Yet, if they just had faith as a mustard seed, willing and yielded to God to grow as a mustard seed grows, they could move mountains. It is the faith of a seed that is totally dependent on God for its growth (Mark 4:26-28). It is faith that is willing to die to what it is in order to become all that it is meant to be. It is faith like a blade of grass that grows up through asphalt or the tiniest crack in concrete. It is the tender shoot that pushes up from under a rock to reach for the sun. It starts small. It is still faith, even though it is small. But, it does not remain small. It grows strong, giving glory to God.

Chapter 8

Our God Does Whatever He Pleases

God's sovereignty must be the basis for our faith and our rest. God is here. He is alive and well and living among us. All good comes from Him. In control of all things, though He doesn't cause it, He allows the bad to come. He would not allow it if He could not use it for our good.

> *"Our God is in the heavens; He does whatever He pleases."*
> Psalm 115:3

After Peter and John were released from prison and returned to their fellow Christians, they "reported all that the chief priests and the elders had said to them." The Christians responded with a prayer. After a brief praise and a reference to the prophecy of Psalm 2:1-2, It continues in Acts 4:27-28 as follows:

> *"For truly in this city, there were gathered together against Your holy servant Jesus, whom You anointed, both Herod and Pontius Pilate, along with the Gentiles and the peoples of Israel, to do whatever Your hand and Your purpose predestined to occur."*

Having thus established the sovereignty of God as a basis for their praying, they make their request that as God continues to work through them, He also be aware of the reactions of those who oppose them, and give His servants confidence to continue to speak His word.

There are here at least two lessons for us. The first is that God is sovereign. He knew what was to happen to Christ, to the point that all those involved in His trial and execution—Herod, Pilate, the Gentiles and the peoples of Israel—were carrying out God's predetermined plan. The second is that we can pray with more confidence when we know that God is in control, carrying out His will for the redemption of man, and including the events of our lives in the redemption process.

God does have a plan. He does have a will. He is going to see that His plan and His will come to pass. He is faithful. "'They will fight against you, but they will not overcome you, for I am with you to deliver you,' declares the Lord" (Jeremiah 1:19). "God is faithful, through whom you were called into fellowship with His Son, Jesus Christ our Lord" (1 Corinthians 1:9). "Faithful is He who calls you, and He also will bring it to pass" (1 Thessalonians 5:24). Let these verses on God's faithfulness encourage you when the storms of life begin to blow. If you believe he is faithful, it will be a source of comfort to you.

> *"No temptation has overtaken you but such as is common to man; and God is faithful, who will not allow you to be tempted beyond what you are able, but with the temptation will provide the way of escape also, so that you may be able to endure it."*
>
> 1 Corinthians 10:13

He is faithful. He will not allow anything to come against you that you cannot bear. The fact that you are facing the situation is proof in itself that it is not unbearable. He is faithful. The fact you are facing the situation is also His promise that He will provide a way of escape. Do you believe this? (It is unfortunate that we do not have a verb form of "faith" in English.) Do you "faith" that He is faithful? Let your faith affect your response to Him and to the situation at hand. Do not fear the storms. Do not be angry with God. He is using the storm to mold you into the image of Christ and to bring praise to Himself. If He could not, He would intervene and deliver you at once. Since He can use it, He will, and see you through it to victory anyway. Trust Him.

Peter was in a boat being battered by waves and high winds when Jesus came walking across the water toward the boat. Why he wanted to get out of the boat is not clear. Maybe because, thinking Jesus was a ghost, he had said, "Lord, if it is You command me to come to You on the water." When the Lord did, Peter, in his pride, may have felt He could not back down. He got out of the boat and walked on water toward Jesus. When he saw the wind, he "became afraid" and began to sink. He cried out to the Lord to save him, and immediately Jesus reached out and took hold of him. "And when they got into the boat, the wind stopped" (Matthew 14:24-32). What happened between Jesus' taking hold of him and their getting into the boat? Apparently, they walked together—on the water, through the waves—back to the boat. Then the wind stopped.

He is faithful. He will reach out and take hold of you. He may not stop the storm until you have walked with Him through it for a while. But He will stop it. He may take you to the place of refuge first, but He will stop it.

One of the reasons we do not understand what God is doing is that we look at our situation "through the wrong end of the binoculars." When you read the great Psalms of hope in the Bible, David often rehearsed what God had done, often beginning from the earliest stories of the Hebrew patriarchs. He would proclaim what God had done on their behalf. Then he would move on to the deliverance of the people from Egypt, God's provision in the wilderness, His leading them into the promised land, and conquering the enemy. Finally, he would review some of the things God had done for him personally. By the time he finally got around to his current situation, God's ability and willingness to hear his cry and answer his prayer was big and bold in his view. It was like looking at something already near through a pair of binoculars and bringing it even closer. His love and provision were so near they were almost overwhelming.

We, on the other hand, look at our present problem and never stop to think how He has delivered us in times past. We are like the apostles when Jesus said they were men of little faith because they did not remember or understand. Any hope or solution seems far, far away, like a distant spot on the horizon through the wrong end of the binoculars.

Now let's take a look through binoculars, New Testament style:

He blessed, chose, predestined. **He** did so according to the kind intention of **His** will. **He** freely bestowed **His** grace on us. It is in **Him** we have redemption through **His** blood and forgiveness according to the riches of **His** grace. **He** lavished **His** grace on us. **He** made known the mystery of **His** will. **He** had a purpose in doing so. **He** acted "with a view to an administration" (with a specific plan in mind). In **Him**, we obtained an inheritance. In **Him**, we have been predestined according to **His** purpose, who works all things after the counsel of **His** will. (Ephesians 1:3-14)

For our purposes here, an indepth treatise on the sovereignty of God is not necessary. It is necessary, though, that a basic understanding and acceptance of His sovereignty be reached.

From Ephesians 1:3-14, it is obvious that God is the "prime mover," or initiator, in the redemption of man. Calvinists may take the passage to support their view that some are predestined to salvation. Others may argue, "No, we who are saved are predestined to adoption through Jesus Christ. The predestination had to do with the predetermined method, not with which individuals would or would not be saved."

Quite frankly, I don't think either of those views is worth dying for. Jesus is worth dying for. The indisputable fact of these scriptures is that God is sovereign. He **does**. He moves; He acts; *He has a plan*. He is not surprised by anyone or anything. "Nothing has ever 'occurred' to God."[1] He finished His work on an eternal timetable (how's that for an oxymoron?). We are *experiencing* it in the framework of space and time. He worked six days, and on the seventh, He rested. He finished His work before the foundation of the world and ceased from His works.

Before we move on from this, please read Ephesians 1:3-14 from your favorite translation. Read it through at least once, and ask God to open your heart to more fully understand its message. There is a wealth of insight to be gained from this passage, of which God's sovereignty is but a part. After you read it, go through it again, praying it back to God.

Let me show you what I mean, but please do not just pray this prayer. Open the scripture for yourself and pray it back to God in your own words. If you are still not sure how, ask the Holy Spirit to guide you.

"God, Father of my Lord Jesus Christ, I bless You. I thank You and honor You for blessing me with every spiritual blessing in the heavens in Christ. I thank You that You have done this in just the same way that You decided before the foundation of the world (before Adam was created, definitely before I was born) that I would be holy and blameless before You. Lord, forgive me for all my foolish efforts at righteousness in my strength when You have said it is Your choice for me, and You have provided the means in Your predetermined plan and strength. Thank You for loving me so much that You chose to make me Your child through Jesus Christ, in direct proportion to Your good pleasure, and to the praise of the glory of Your grace. Thank You for graciously gracing me with Your grace (freely and abundantly lavishing Your grace on me) in the Beloved. Thank You that in Him and through His blood, I have redemption, the forgiveness of my sins, in proportion to the riches of Your grace, which You lavished upon me. (Lord, if You have so much grace that You can dole it out lavishly and extravagantly, that must mean the forgiveness of my sins is just as abundant. Hallelujah! Glory to God!) Thank You for revealing to me this plan, hidden through the ages, but to which all history points. It pleases You to graciously forgive men and restore them to Yourself in Christ so that in Your divine economy, all things will add up in Christ. Thank You for the inheritance which I received through the death of Jesus (not through my death, but His death), that all things are summed up in Christ, and all things add up to Your predetermined purpose of molding me into the image of Christ, to the end that I exist 'to the praise of YOUR glory.' Thank You, that I, having believed the gospel of my salvation, have been sealed by You with the Holy Spirit of promise, as an earnest of my inheritance. Thank You for putting Your Holy Spirit on the line in this way, that if You do not come through with my inheritance, then You lose the earnest which You put up as proof of payment. Since you cannot lose the Spirit, I must have a pretty sure thing going. There can be no doubt that the inheritance You promise is mine. Lord, with this assurance, let me live in faith in You in such a way that my living will contribute to the redemption of Your possession and to the praise of Your glory. Amen."

Note the three times that Paul pointed out that God's actions were for the praise of His glory. If God is indeed the supreme being in the whole universe, then He is of the highest value. For us to act for the praise of our own glory would be conceit. But for God to not act for the praise of His glory would deny His own worth and would in fact be idolatrous. There is no greater gift He can give us than Himself. This is the basis of all of redemption history. It is supreme love, for there is nothing greater He can offer to His creation. "What could God give us to enjoy that would prove him most loving? There is only one possible answer: himself. If he withholds himself from our contemplation and companionship, no matter what else he gives us, he is not loving."[2]

God is a loving God. He offers us entry into the holy of holies: the privilege of always living in His presence. He is sovereign. He does whatever He pleases. He is willing to accept responsibility for good and bad because ultimately, He is fully in control of all things. If He were not that powerful, He would not be God. He is worthy of our trust.

Chapter 9

God's Purpose

The Good for Which All Things Work Together

Yes, "all things." You can hear it coming: Romans 8:28 says: 'All things work together for good to them that love the Lord.'" That is the way we usually hear it quoted. This verse is very casually tossed about by well-meaning Christians to comfort one another, especially when the situation does not directly affect the speaker. I am convinced very few of us anywhere near fully grasp the depth of meaning in this passage.

"Just as our joy is based on the promise that God is strong enough and wise enough to make all things work together for our good, so God's joy is based on that same sovereign control: He makes all things work together for His glory."[1]

God's purpose for our lives goes far beyond a task, a ministry, or even a calling. His purpose is to mold us into the image of His Son so that we may be able to fellowship with Him as intimately as His own Son does. This is an eternal goal. It is a far greater priority than anything we may do in the temporal, earthly realm.

"God created man in His image, in the image of God He created him; male and female He created them. God blessed them; and God said to them, 'Be fruitful and multiply, and fill the earth, and subdue it; and rule over the fish of the sea and the birds of the sky, and over every living thing that moves on the earth'" (Genesis 1:27-28). We were created in God's image. His purpose from the beginning was for us to be like Him. The fall interrupted God's purpose and made redemption necessary. The fall separated us from God, His image, and the dominion we were to have over all the earth.

The Psalmist, in awe, that the God who created everything somehow considers man important and worthy to even be thought of by God, says, "You make him to rule over the works of Your hands; You have put all things under his feet" (Psalm 8:6). The writer of Hebrews, referring to this, says, "For in subjecting all things to him [man], He [God] left nothing that is not subject to him [man]. But now we do not yet see all things subjected to him [man]. But we do see Him who was made for a little while lower than the angels, namely, Jesus, because of the suffering of death crowned with glory and honor" (Heb.2:8-9). We read in Ephesians 1 how God had a plan, to sum up all things in Christ in the fullness of times. We saw how this plan would bring glory to God and praise to the glory of His grace. It would gloriously demonstrate that God's plan of redemption and sanctification could be attributed to nothing but the absolute grace of God. Coming to the cross, Jesus prayed, "Father, the hour has come; glorify Your Son, that the Son may glorify You" (John 17:1). Wow! Do you see it?

How did the Father glorify the Son? "We see ... Jesus, because of the suffering of death crowned with glory and honor." When did He do it? When the time was right, in the fullness of time. Ephesians 1:10 is NOT some event yet to take place. Jesus said, "The hour has come." The time was full, and in His death, God summed up all things in Christ, making Him heir of **all things** (Hebrews 1:2), and making His cross our cross (Romans 6:5-8), He adopted us as sons and made us joint-heirs with Christ (Romans 8:17). That is joint-heirs. We inherit the **same** thing He did. Which was **All things**.

No, we may still not see all things subjected under the feet of man. We still see Jesus. In Him, God has worked out a plan so that all things become our inheritance. Good or bad, large or small, all things are turned to the working out of God's good purpose in our lives: to conform us to the image of His Son. What image is that? "He is the radiance of His glory and the exact representation of His nature" (Hebrews 1:3). What we know of the sun is what it radiates to us over millions of miles—light and warmth. What we know of God is what He radiates to us—His Son. What the world knows of the Son will largely be through us as we are conformed to His image.

EXTREME Gratitude

How do we do this? How do I become like Christ? It is found throughout the Bible: we look at Jesus. Consider Jesus. Set your mind on things above, not on things on the earth. Seek first the kingdom of God and His righteousness. That I may know Him. That is your part—to know Him.

Do you make yourself holy? "Therefore you are to be perfect, as your heavenly Father is perfect" (Matthew 5:48). By grace, you are saved through faith, and that not of yourselves, it is the gift of God; not as a result of works lest anyone should boast. He who began a good work in you will complete it. It is God who is at work both to will and to work for His good pleasure. As you have received Christ Jesus (by grace through faith, not of works), so walk in Him. By His doing you are in Christ Jesus, who became to us wisdom from God, and righteousness and sanctification and redemption, that, just as it is written, "Let him who boasts, boast in the Lord." It is His pleasure to effect our redemption through Jesus Christ. It is His good pleasure to work out in us His will. What He wills, He performs. What He commands, He does.

Our part is faith. Our part is trust. This is humbling. There is nothing we can do. When He says, "Humble yourself," He is not talking about just being a humble person. He is saying "Humble yourself under the mighty hand of God ... casting all your anxiety upon Him because He cares for you." How do you humble yourself? You cast all your anxiety upon Him and rest in the fact that He cares for you. There is nothing for you to do in your strength or ability.

In your heart, mix faith with this word, "All Things," and enter a new level of rest.

When trials come, if you know He has given even this thing into your hands as your inheritance, you will trust Him. You will be able to "consider it all joy" (James 1:2). You will exult in your tribulations as much as you do in hope of the glory of God (Rom.5:3-5). You will realize that God is using even this for the purpose of molding you into the image of His Son.

Where do our troubles and tribulation come from? I heard someone say recently that there are three sources: 1) God, 2) Satan, 3) the result of our being outside the will of God. Ultimately, God, being sovereign, is quite willing to take responsibility. No, God does not cause divorce. That comes as the result of human sin and failure. It comes, however, with deep pain. If there were no pain involved, we would not think twice about divorcing our partner or raise the question as to why it happens. That pain is from God. He does not wait until we turn it over to Him to use it. From the very first twinge, it is His chastisement making us aware that we are outside of His will and in need of Him. It is the call of a loving Father to turn again to "consider Him" (Hebrews 12:3).

He does not kill. Jesus identified Satan as the one who comes to steal, kill, and destroy (John 10:10). He also said He took on flesh and blood to render of no effect "him who had the power of death, that is the devil" (Hebrews 2:14). Will I still die? Yes, but for me, to die is gain (Philippians 1:21). There is no horror there. Death has lost its sting. For those left behind, there is loss and loneliness. But these feelings, too, are reminders of the fact that He alone can ultimately fill and satisfy our hearts, and He alone will never forsake us or leave us.

Does He cause sickness? Let me try to avoid a direct answer to that one, and give you an example of Job instead. Someone once told me there were three types of sickness in the Bible. One was "the sickness to the glory of God." Another was "sickness unto death." The third was "sickness for chastisement." After hearing this, I dove headlong into the Word to verify it. The only examples I found of the first one were incidents where God was glorified by the healing of the sick person. The only place a "sickness unto death" is mentioned is John 11, where Jesus says that Lazarus' illness "is not unto death, but for the glory of God." What happened? Lazarus died. But that was not the end. He was raised from the dead "that the Son of God may be glorified by it."

EXTREME *Gratitude*

I remembered the story of Job. I read the whole book. Satan went to God and asked permission to afflict Job. He killed Job's oxen, donkeys, sheep, servants, and children, then afflicted him with boils and with a wife who told him to curse God and die. Job's response to her was, "Shall we indeed accept good from God and not accept adversity?" The verse concludes, "In all this Job did not sin with his lips" (Job 2:10). God gave him "friends" who accused him of having sinned and of having thereby incurred the wrath of God. Job defended his righteousness against the accusations of his friends. However, Job himself said, "I loathe my own life; I will give full vent to my complaint; I will speak in the bitterness of my soul. I will say to God, 'Do not condemn me; let me know why You contend with me. Is it right for You indeed to oppress, to reject the labor of Your hands, and to look favorably on the schemes of the wicked? ... According to Your knowledge I am indeed not guilty; yet there is no deliverance from Your hand?'" (Job 10:1-3, 7). Did God get upset with Job for blaming Him for his troubles? No, He was angry with Job's friends because they had "not spoken of Me what is right **as My servant Job** has" (Job 42:7). God was fully willing to take responsibility for Job's problems, even though Satan was the one who had carried out the deeds against Job.

Here are some lessons from Job.

1. God is sovereign. He is comfortable with His sovereignty to the point that He is willing to take responsibility even for the things Satan does. Job 42:11 says Job's brothers and sisters "consoled and comforted him for all the adversity that the Lord had brought on him."

2. God gave Job the freedom to fully vent his complaint, and both have and speak the bitterness of his soul. To say God is sovereign and He is using all things, and we should trust Him and give thanks, does not negate the pain we will feel. It does not mean we will not feel angry toward God. It does not mean we may not complain to God about His seeming lack

of interest. Job said, "If I called and He answered me, I could not believe that He was listening to my voice" (9:16). We may have these same feelings. God is sovereign enough to handle that, too. However, we must move on, eventually, leaving these feelings behind and moving into faith and thanksgiving.

3. Job longed for death, but held on until he finally reached a point of saying, "I know that You can do all things and that no purpose of Yours can be thwarted … Therefore I retract, and I repent in dust and ashes" (42:2-6).

4. God used the tragedies in Job's life to increase his knowledge of God, increase his faith, and increase his awareness of his weakness and need to trust God fully.

5. When Job finally submitted to the hand of God in his life, God used him to intercede for his judgmental friends.

A friend of mine said, regarding some of the struggles he is facing, "I don't know what God is trying to do in my life; where all this is leading me." My first thought was, "Sure you do. He wants to mold you into the image of His Son." Then the Lord reminded me of the process I am going through to get to where I understand this, and for Him to make it my first and normal response to the struggles and challenges in my own life. (I'm still on the journey.)

As I described in the introduction, at nine, I first felt the call to "full-time Christian vocational service." By the age of 13, I believed that to be foreign missions. The week after graduation from high school I led music in revival services at Levy Street Mission in Shreveport. The joy with which these people, in a very poor neighborhood of town, sang and worshipped really blessed me. The next Sunday, in my home church, as we sang the hymns, for some reason, I looked around. The faces all looked cold, dead, and disinterested. The Lord seemed to say, "I don't need you in foreign missions. There is plenty for you to do right here in this country."

So, I went to college, thinking I was preparing for the pastorate. I majored in religion and minored in Greek and sociology. During my junior year, I began working as Chaplain's assistant at Central Louisiana State (mental) Hospital. As I saw the fine line between "sanity" and mental illness, I realized that many of the patients could have been spared the stigma of being in a mental hospital had there only been a pastor who would have shared with them along the way even some basic mental, emotional, and spiritual truths to help them deal more effectively with the situations they faced in life.

I finished college in December 1974, and headed to seminary, convinced counseling would be a major part of my ministry. That first year I worked for a small company that was writing alcohol and drug education programs to be used in the public school system. What I learned there, along with my previous experience in counseling, landed me a job at a drug treatment center for narcotics addicts. I spent two years working with people who had little desire for, or in some cases, a great fear of change, even for the better. In August 1977, I took a job in a fledgling Christian book store chain, mainly because of the opportunities to counsel and pray with people. I went from clerk to assistant manager to store manager to the warehouse manager for a sister company. From there, I became field representative for the home office of the chain, then leasing agent.

I had experienced God's call and had a strong sense of purpose in my life. All through these years, I could see how one job led to another. I was aware of how God was growing me and teaching me. Yet I found myself from time to time wondering how what I was doing fit in to His call. I longed to see a ministry to street people like those at the drug treatment center. There were a lot of ministries evangelizing on the streets. My vision was to take these new born babes that no one knew what to do with, or wanted nothing to do with, and help them grow in the Lord.

Then the opportunity came to "buy" the two stores I had previously managed by assuming the current franchisee's debts. I was young and inexperienced enough not to realize that a business can show a profit and still be insolvent. Because of my understanding of the merchandising and operations of the stores, friends and coworkers were telling me, "If anyone can make this work, you can." Here it was. God's plan was unfolding. First these two stores. Then, eventually, two or three more. These would provide enough income to support the ministry as well as provide a place for the clients to work as they were beginning to get their lives back in order. It made such perfect sense, in my thinking.

All through the years, I had been seeking a task, a calling, a ministry, i.e., "God's purpose in my life." Long before, I had accepted the truth of Romans 8:28-29. And now it seemed to be taking shape. However, I was still looking for "God's purpose" in things that were temporal.

As it turned out, **nobody** "could make this work." We watched the business crumble around us for a year before we finally had to close it down in December 1982. I had so intensely believed this was a part of God's calling in my life that I had poured myself into this chain of stores for over five years. It was like the departure of a loved one to whom you have committed your life—whether through death or divorce. When they go, they take part of you with them. Not only did I lose a big piece of myself, but suddenly, everything I was working toward was gone. There was no purpose.

God had stripped away everything to which I was clinging as part of His purpose for my life, in order to let me see what His purpose was. The principle is set forth in 2 Corinthians 4:7, 10, 16-18:

> *"But we have this treasure in earthen vessels, so that the surpassing greatness of the power may be of God and not from ourselves ... always carrying about in the body*

> *the dying of Jesus, so that the life of Jesus also may be manifested in our body ... Therefore we do not lose heart, but though our outer man is decaying, yet our inner man is being renewed day by day. For momentary, light affliction is producing for us an eternal weight of glory far beyond all comparison, while we look not at the things which are seen, but at the things which are not seen; for the things which are seen are temporal, but the things which are not seen are eternal."*

Not everything that is real can be seen with the eyes. The "most real" things are the eternal. They are the only things that will last, and they cannot be seen with the eyes.

Hear Andrew Murray's admonition:

> "I will tell you where you fail. You have never yet heartily believed that He was working out your salvation. You believe that if a painter undertakes a picture, he must look to every shade of color and every touch upon the canvas. You believe that if a workman makes a table or a bench, he knows how to do his work. But you do not believe that the everlasting God is working out the image of His Son in you. As any sister here is doing a piece of ornamental or fancy work, following out the pattern in every detail, let her just think: 'Can God not work out in me the purpose of His love?' If that piece of work is to be perfect, every stitch must be in its place. And remember that not one minute of your life should be without God. We want God to come in at times—say in the morning; then we are to live two or three hours, and He can come in again. No, God must be every moment the Worker in your soul."[2]

We tend to think of God's purpose for our lives in terms of "ministry." We think His purpose has to do with our "calling" or vocation. This is especially true when it comes to "the" ministry—serving Him professionally. However, God's purpose is so much higher than this. We tend to limit our understanding of purpose to the temporal, what we do while on earth.

God's purpose is to mold us into the image of Christ. His purpose is to make us holy by becoming our wisdom, righteousness, sanctification, and redemption. His purpose is to bring us to faith—absolute certainty in His trustworthiness. His purpose is to bring us to the end of our labor, our effort, and lead us into our Sabbath rest—total dependence on and acceptance of His work on our behalf. His purpose is to bring us to faith in His ability, desire, and determination to accomplish His purpose in and through us by His strength and not our own. His purpose is to teach us **the message of the cross—through our death with Christ on His cross the very power of God Himself is set loose to accomplish His redemptive work in us and through us**. Praise be to God!

Chapter 10

God's Purpose Continued

The Praise and Glory of His Grace

Look again at these words from John Piper:

> "Just as our joy is based on the promise that God is strong enough and wise enough to make all things work together for our good, so God's joy is based on that same sovereign control: He makes all things work together for His glory."1

His glory—the One who, alone, deserves glory. We are predestined to adoption through Jesus "to the praise of the glory of His grace." We have obtained an inheritance "to the end that we … should be to the praise of His glory." He has given His Spirit as a pledge of our inheritance "to the praise of His glory." We are predestined to this inheritance. To make sure we received it, He adopted us as sons through Jesus Christ and sealed us with His Holy Spirit. The purpose for giving us this inheritance is "the praise of His glory" (Ephesians 1:5-6, 11-12, 13-14).

The One who predestined us to this inheritance is the One who works *all things* after the counsel of His will. This works for us because Jesus is *heir of all things* (Heb.1:2), and we are joint-heirs with Christ (Romans 8:17). We have been qualified, by His doing, to share in the inheritance of the saints (Colossians 1:12). He enables us to know the riches of the glory of His inheritance in the saints in light (Ephesians 1:18).

What is "the inheritance of the saints in light?" He has made us a royal priesthood, a people for God's possession, calling us out of darkness into His marvelous light.

> *"But you are a chosen race, a royal priesthood, a holy nation, a people for God's possession, so that you may proclaim the*

excellencies of Him who has called you out of darkness into His marvelous light; for you once were not a people, but now you are the people of God; you had not received mercy, but now you have received mercy."
                                                                     1 Peter 2:9-10

"For by Him, all things were created … all things have been created through Him and for Him. He is before all things, and in Him, all things hold together … firstborn from the dead; so that He Himself will come to have first place in everything. For it was the Father's good pleasure … through Him to reconcile all things to Himself, having made peace through the blood of His cross …" (Colossians 1:16-20). As a result, all things are subject to Him (Hebrews 2:8). **All things** are under His authority and subject to His will because all things were created for Him and by Him, and He has first place in everything. Through the cross of Calvary and the blood of the lamb, God took delight in reconciling all things to Himself.

In all things, God works to mold us into the image of His Son. The result is our being enabled to do His will. This is grace. It is the enabling of God's people through the power of "Christ in you, the hope of glory" (Colossians 1:27). As you see His grace spread through your life by means of all things, give thanks to God, for in so doing you will bring glory to God. But this will only happen in you when you really trust Him to be using **all things**. "For all things are for your sakes, so that the grace which is spreading … may cause the giving of thanks to abound to the glory of God" (2 Corinthians 4:15).

It is important to make sure we are properly defining "all things." We tend to emphasize the word "things" and assume this means all the tangible, material things we can experience with our senses. As a result, we think that the good which God works all things together to accomplish is something tangible. We, therefore, translate it: "All things work out for the best." This is why we sometimes don't understand how God is going to use "this" for our good, or what good will come out of this. The emphasis of scripture appears to be on the word "ALL." It includes, indeed emphasizes, eternal things. It is the word "all" that brings the spiritual emphasis to the work God is doing in us to mold us into His image and bring praise and glory to Himself.

God's grace has a cyclical function and effect. For He is reconciling all things to Himself in order to give all things to His heirs for the maturing of them into the image of His Son. It is learning how to go on the way you got in. As you do, others will see how to get in by the way you go on, and thereby be reconciled to God. "Now all these things are from God, who reconciled us to Himself through Christ, and gave us the ministry of reconciliation" (2 Corinthians 5:18). It is with a view to reconciling all men to Himself that He has sealed us with His own Holy Spirit as both the proof and the promise of our inheritance (Ephesians 1:13-14).

To reconcile means to restore to friendship. It means to so thoroughly put away all enmity that friendship follows.[2] It is the process whereby He gives us His righteousness so that we may be qualified recipients of the love He wants to give us. We do not deserve His love, so He makes us deserving of it. It is by His doing that we are in Christ Jesus (1 Corinthians 1:30-31), not having a righteousness of our own, but that which is through faith in Christ (Philippians 3:9). It is the mystery of the ages now revealed, Christ in you, the hope of glory (Colossians 1:26-27). It is an expression of His grace, lavished upon us, to the praise of the glory of His grace (Ephesians 1:6-8). The "Minister of Reconciliation" is not the title of yet another professional Christian. The ministry of reconciliation is the task given to us by Jesus in the great commission: to introduce others to His plan of restoring man to Himself. In ministering His reconciliation to our world, we fulfill His "household" economy of summing up all things in Christ and redeeming His purchased, blood-bought possession to Himself, to the praise of His glory.

He delights in blessing us. He delights in reconciling men to Himself through His Son Jesus Christ. He takes great joy in us. He desires that we take as much joy in Him and introduce others to the joy of finding joy in Him.

In 2 Corinthians 1:11, Paul gives an additional insight into God's use of all things, including suffering, to bring honor to Himself. Concluding his teachings that suffering trains us to depend on God and that as God comforts us in our suffering, we are thereby equipped to comfort others, Paul concludes: "And you can help us with your prayers. Then many people will give thanks for us—that God blessed us because of their many prayers" (2 Corinthians 1:11 NCV). From this, first, we see that our prayers do have an effect. It is important to intercede for others, particularly those involved in spreading the gospel because our prayers will actually help them in their work. Beyond this, though, Paul is saying that when you pray for someone and they are helped by your prayers, you should give thanks to God. As more participate in the ministry by praying, then more people are involved, also, in giving thanks, and the honor given to God is increased.

As we move on, we will look more closely at the concept of giving thanks for all things.

Chapter 11

Extreme Thanks

Giving Thanks Always for All Things

The pastor at the church I attended as a boy, preached one Sunday from the passage, "In everything give thanks; for this is God's will for you in Christ Jesus" (1 Thessalonians 5:18). He made it very clear that the passage says *in everything*, not *for* everything. He emphasized this with the illustration, "If you were in a car wreck, you would not thank God for the wreck. You might thank Him that you were not hurt as badly as you might have been, that the wreck was not as bad as it could have been, but you would not thank Him for the wreck itself."

I've run across a lot of Bible verses that contain a command to give thanks. The passage may have nothing to do with praise or thanksgiving, yet, suddenly, there it is, smack in the middle of a perfectly good scripture passage, some seemingly unrelated admonition to give thanks.

The more I encountered these, the more I began to realize that all the lessons God had been teaching me through the years about various aspects of the Christian life were part of a unified whole. The relationship between them is broad, but this was the thread that first began pulling them together. Look through some of them for yourself and let God begin to work them into your spirit.

2 Corinthians 4:10-15 talks about the effect of the cross in the lives of believers in bringing us into the life of Christ. Verse 15 says:

> *"For **all things** are for your sakes, that the grace which is spreading to more and more people may cause the **giving of thanks** to abound to the glory of God."*

2 Corinthians 9:8-12 tells about the collection of money by the believers in Corinth to help the believers in Jerusalem. Paul tells them that God will give them an abundance, enriching them so that they can more abundantly bless others. He says in verse 12, "For the ministry of this service is not only fully supplying the needs of the saints but is also **overflowing through many thanksgivings to God**."

Ephesians 5:3-4 deals with purity in lifestyle and speech, saying "there must be no filthiness and silly talk, or coarse jesting, which are not fitting, but rather **giving of thanks**."

Philippians 4:6-7 states, "Be anxious for nothing, but in everything by prayer and supplication **with thanksgiving**, let your requests be made known to God. And the peace of God, which surpasses all comprehension, will guard your hearts and your minds in Christ Jesus."

Colossians 1:9-13 is a prayer that you will know the will of God in all spiritual wisdom and understanding. One result requested in this prayer is our being "strengthened with all power, according to His glorious might, for the attaining of all steadfastness and patience; **joyously giving thanks** to the Father, who has qualified us to share in the inheritance of the saints in light. For He rescued us from the domain of darkness and transferred us to the kingdom of His beloved Son."

Colossians 2:6-7 says, "Therefore as you have received Christ Jesus the Lord, so walk in Him, having been firmly rooted and now being built up in Him and established in your faith, just as you were instructed and **overflowing with gratitude**."

Colossians 3:15-17 tells us, "Let the peace of Christ rule in your hearts, to which you were called in one body; **and be thankful**. Let the word of Christ richly dwell within you, with all wisdom teaching and admonishing one another with psalms and hymns and spiritual songs, singing **with thankfulness** in your hearts to God. Whatever you do in word or deed, do all in the name of the Lord Jesus, **giving thanks through Him** to God the Father."

EXTREME *Gratitude*

1 Thessalonians 5:16-18 commands, "Rejoice always; pray without ceasing; in everything **give thanks**; for this is God's will for you in Christ Jesus."

1 Timothy 2:1 encourages, "First of all, then, I urge that entreaties and prayers, petitions and **thanksgivings**, be made on behalf of all men."

The clincher for me was Ephesians 5:20, "always giving thanks for all things in the name of our Lord Jesus Christ to God, even the Father."

I had heard "*in* everything, but not *for* everything." But here it is in the scripture: "**giving thanks for all things**." It says it and means it. Think of all the "what abouts" you can. What about the pink slip from work? Bankruptcy? What about the rebellious attitude of my children? What about my broken arm? What about that car wreck? What about divorce? What about being unjustly blamed? What about drug addiction? Adultery? What about sexual abuse? What about child abuse? What about my child's diabetes? What about cancer? What about a global pandemic?

All of these things and any others you came up with are part of "all things" in your life. Jesus is heir of all things. You are joint heir with Him. All things that happen in your life, all the things you do, all the things that are done to you, all things are given to Him to be used to the praise and glory of His grace and for the purpose of molding you into the image of His Son. There is nothing that is not included.

"No temptation [test, trial] has overtaken you but such as is common to man; and God is faithful, who will not allow you to be tempted beyond what you are able, but with the temptation will provide the way of escape also, so that you may be able to endure it" (1 Corinthians 10:13). God is faithful. You can trust Him. He knows what you can and cannot bear, and what He can and cannot use in your life to accomplish His purposes. He does not promise we will not face temptation, persecution, testing, trouble. He does promise it will not exceed the limits of what we can bear, and He does promise a way out.

Here are some corollaries.

1. If you are facing, or have faced, a given problem or temptation, it is proof that it is not more than you can bear, even if there are times you feel like it is. To say, "This is more than I can bear," is to call God a liar. It is also to agree with the father of lies. True, there are some things you *cannot bear in your strength*! The lesson here is that He is faithful, and there is nothing you will face that you cannot bear because He will make a way out so that you can bear it.

2. You can have confidence that the situation or temptation you are facing will never go beyond the limits of your endurance.

3. If God could not in any way use a given situation in your life, you will never have to face that situation.

4. The fact that you have experienced what you have (rape, abuse, neglect, whatever), done what you did (drugs, divorce, abortion, adultery, pornography, foul language, bad temper, whatever), etc., is proof that God can use and is using those very things to mold you into the image of Christ.

5. Not only is there a way out of temptation, but since that word can also be translated "tested" or "tried," however, you see your situation, there is a way out. You do not forever have to remain in bondage to the hurts and scars of your past, whether inflicted upon you or self-inflicted.

Giving thanks for some of the things listed above may seem contrary to all you have ever been taught, but stay with me on this one. This is the hope of healing and liberty you have been looking for.

EXTREME Gratitude

"For the wrath of God is revealed from heaven against all ungodliness and unrighteousness of men, who suppress the truth in unrighteousness. ... For since the creation of the world His invisible attributes, His eternal power, and divine nature, have been clearly seen, being understood through what has been made, so that they are without excuse."

Romans 1:18-20

The implication is that if they had believed the message of creation and accepted the creator God as God, instead of worshipping His creation, they could have been godly and righteous. If they had looked at the beauty of the world around them, all its intricacies, all its detail, and said this is evidence of a creator God, and worshipped Him as God, they would have been saved. Even though they could have, no man ever has. Instead, "For even though they knew God, they did not honor Him as God, or give thanks ..." (Romans 1:21). Instead, they began to speculate about what all this meant and where it all came from. They professed themselves to be wise. As a result, they became fools with darkened hearts. They traded in the glory of God for darkness, and instead of worshipping eternal God they worshipped temporal man, and animals, and other parts of the creation—none of which will last. God does not force them to love Him, so He gives them up to pursue their self-made religions to their logical conclusions, and they wind up with all kinds of sin and indecency, from disobedience to parents, to greed, to arrogance, to homosexuality, to envy, to murder, and on and on goes the list.

The heart of this passage is in verse 21: "They did not honor Him as God, or give thanks." The purpose of all things is to bring glory to God. We are to always give thanks for all things. To not give thanks is not to believe that He is God in the area of your life you are refusing to thank Him for. Giving thanks for all things demonstrates that I trust God. He is God, He is faithful, and He will use the chaos of life for the highest purposes possible—to bring praise and glory to Himself and to mold me into the image of Christ.

What is this image of Christ we have been talking about? He came in total dependence upon the Father. He did only what He saw the Father doing. He said only what He heard the Father saying. We are exhorted to have His mind, which did not seek after the glory that was rightfully His, being God, but humbled Himself in obedience to the point of death. He submitted totally to the will of the Father (Philippians 2:5-11). Then He said, "As the Father has sent me, I also send you" (John 20:21). There is that word "as" again. In the same manner (total dependence on Him) that the Father sent Jesus, Jesus sends us (total dependence on Him).

In the sense that molding us into the image of Christ means getting rid of the fleshly character traits and garments of the old nature we may still be wearing around, this process can be seen as chastisement. It may not be for some specific sin such as lying, stealing, adultery, coveting, dishonoring your parents, or breaking other commandments of the law. It may be for a more hideous sin, such as not trusting a loving and trustworthy God.

Take a minute and read the twelfth chapter of Hebrews. We must lay aside like old clothes, the things that entangle us, and keep us from running the race that is before us. When it gets tough, and the temptations are fierce, and the pain is deep and burning, consider (that means think deeply about) Jesus. He endured the cross. He hung on two pieces of wood, probably getting splinters in His already scourged, torn, and bleeding back, with nails through His arms and feet, with long sharp thorns digging into His scalp for about six hours. He had nothing to eat since the day before, and nothing to drink. He was stripped and hung up to die a humiliating death before a crowd of people. To be executed this way indicated He had committed a serious crime. But He was sinless. He endured the humiliation and death you and I deserved, and died for our sins. He endured the cross. In your striving against sin in your own life, have you resisted to the point of shedding blood? Or are you bucking against the discipline of the Lord, which for a season is quite unpleasant, but will produce in you the very righteousness, peace, strength, and sanctification (holiness) that you desire?

Some of the "What-abouts" we mentioned earlier were very painful things. Some of you reading this have experienced those pains. In what I have said, and in what I'm about to say, please hear this: When wounds are deep, you are going to feel hurt, physically and emotionally, and probably anger, and maybe an array of other feelings. This is normal. However, it isn't normal or good if you stay there. "See to it that no one comes short of the grace of God; that no root of bitterness springing up causes trouble, and by it many be defiled; that there be no immoral or godless person like Esau who sold his birthright for a meal."

One of the things the Covid-19 pandemic revealed was all the things we think are important that we can do without. We were force to "shelter at home" for several weeks. Many could not go to work, and many of those lost their jobs. Some could work from home, but life was different for everyone. Frankly, it got kind of boring. Possessions, favorite activities, all the things we were used to filling our lives with lost their luster. We had been selling our birthright to settle for the things that would feed our appetites, and they turned out to be empty, meaningless and less than satisfying.

God has grace for every situation. He has dying grace for a dying day. He has cancer grace (and radiation and chemo grace). He has grace for when my baby is crying, and "I don't know why grace" when I do not know. He has rape grace. He has incest grace. He has abuse grace. He has I failed miserably grace. He has out of work grace. Do not fall short of that grace. It is your way out. The way to grasp the grace is by gratitude. To refuse the grace, is to refuse to embrace Him. To refuse His grace is to hold on to the hurt, and that results in bitterness, and more pain, and more defilement. To refuse the grace will result in looking for other ways to ease the pain; like Esau you will grasp something the world offers. Since the world will someday end, that's like giving up the eternal for the temporary. It's giving up your birthright for a meal. It is wicked to trust God so little.

You see, you have not come to Mt. Sinai, where Moses went up to get the law, and the voice of God speaking to Moses was so awesome that the people requested He stop speaking out loud. No, instead of the mountain of the law, you have come to Mt. Zion. The city there is the one Jeremiah spoke of when he foretold the coming of the righteous Branch of David saying, "Jerusalem will dwell in safety; and this is the name by which she will be called; the Lord is our righteousness" (Jeremiah 33:16). The righteousness of God Himself is the city He has given us to dwell in. He has brought us to Himself, to dwell in His presence with Jesus Christ as mediator of a new covenant based on our being sprinkled clean by the blood of the lamb to enter into His presence and abide there forever.

Even so, there is a warning. Just as the earth shook when God spoke, giving the law at Sinai, He will shake the earth again, and only those things that are eternal will remain. What are you holding on to? When the shaking comes in your life, if you are not holding on to Him, you will be left holding on to nothing, because "created things" will be removed.

I am not suggesting that child abuse, rape, incest, or any of these other hideous sins of men are God's methods of chastising people. Those things are sins of men, birthed out of evil, lustful hearts of men who neither glorify God as God nor give thanks. I am saying that if you have experienced any of these things, they are part of the "all things" of your life. And, God can use them to help you let go of things that will not last anyway, and learn to embrace Him. There is nothing else to hold on to that is dependable. There is no one else as trustworthy. Only the eternal will remain stable through shaking as severe as what you have experienced.

> *"Therefore, since we receive a kingdom which cannot be shaken, let us **show gratitude**, by which we may offer to*

EXTREME *Gratitude*

God an acceptable service with reverence and awe;
for our God is a consuming fire."
Hebrews 12:28-29

Whether it is a gentle, or even firm chastisement from the hand of a loving heavenly Father, or cruel defilement from the heart of sinful man (even an earthly father), when entrusted to the God who is faithful, the results are the same, a kingdom which cannot be shaken. Therefore, the response should ultimately be the same, "always giving thanks for all things."

God must be accepted as God. "God" is sovereign. He is all-powerful, all-knowing, all-sufficient, all mighty, final authority. He is in control. Nothing happens without His final approval. Nothing surprises Him. The psalmist declares, "Ascribe to the Lord glory and strength. Ascribe to the Lord the glory due His name" (Psalm 29:1-2). We can bring glory to God by praising Him just for who He is, by proclaiming Him before others and by living in a manner worthy of Him. Quite frankly, though, most of us find it easier to praise Him than to thank Him. Yet, the absence of either one indicates that we are rejecting His complete role as God in our life.

In the two preceding chapters, we looked at "all things." First, we looked at His use of all things to grow and mature us. Then we looked at His using all things to bring praise and glory to Himself. Do you want to be molded into the image of Christ? Do you want God to be glorified in your life? If these are the results of everything that happens to you, then you are getting what you want, right? So, why not thank Him? If that sounds trite, please forgive me, but it is just about that simple (not easy, but simple). If you do trust Him to be sovereignly in control of all things, then you can thank Him for all things. Giving thanks is giving verbal expression to your faith and confidence in God. Thanksgiving is the doorway into faith and the purest, simplest expression of faith.

This is extreme gratitude. It makes no sense when you first hear about it. It makes no sense when you first attempt it. It is easier to express an "attitude of gratitude" in a generic sense - saying thank you to others for kindnesses. It is easy to just say the words "Thank You, Lord" without really saying or even considering what it is you are saying thank you for. It is not too hard to say thank you because "it could have been worse." It is perhaps a little bit of a challenge to begin to look for good things in a bad situation for which you might be thankful. When you try to be thankful for the bad situation itself, it feels almost hypocritical. It is much harder, and the words may not even come out at first. How can you be thankful for something you totally detest? That's just a little too extreme!

Yet when you begin to wrap your mind around the principles we have shared up to this point, you will see that level of gratitude has value. It is the expression of the level of extreme faith an extreme God deserves. When you know that this extreme God extremely loves you and lavishes His grace and love on you to the extreme, how can you say no? He is so worthy of your love in return. He is worthy of your trust, your faith. He is worthy of your extreme faith, and your extreme gratitude.

Chapter 12

Extreme Benefits

The Power of Giving Thanks for All Things

So why does any of this matter? Why should you give thanks? Why should you invest spiritual energy in the idea of giving thanks always for all things? In other words, "What's in it for me? What are the benefits?" The answer to that is found in those "random" verses that we looked at earlier that mention giving thanks. They are like the field in the parable of the kingdom, in which a man found a treasure, hid it again, and from joy over it, he sold everything he had in order to buy that field.

So, why buy into this?

1. **To not do so reveals a lack of faith and opens the door to sin; to do so keeps my focus and faith on Him** (Romans 1).

> *"For even though they knew God, they did not honor Him as God or give thanks, but they became futile in their speculations, and their foolish heart was darkened."*
> Romans 1:21

We've looked at this passage already. It deals with the failure to give thanks, and shows the horrible depths of sin into which men fall when they refuse to give thanks to God. They are not acknowledging Him as God, giving Him the honor He is due, placing their faith in His existence, His power, or His love. They do not believe that He truly is, nor do they believe that He is a rewarder of those who seek Him. If they did "faith" that He is and that He is a rewarder, they would find great joy in these truths, rejoice and be thankful to Him for who He is and what He does. They would know that because He truly cares for them, He will watch over and protect them and have their best interests at heart. They would love Him, seek to draw near Him, abide in His love and embrace, and honor Him with heart, soul, mind, and strength. It would spill over into their relationships with others around them, both the saved and the lost—their brethren and their neighbors.

So, the flip side of it is this. If not being thankful opens the door to futility and darkened hearts, then being thankful opens the door to overwhelming victory, life, holiness, and light.

2. **It recognizes what He has done for me, giving a foundation for me to seek and know His will** (Colossians 1).

> *"... strengthened with all power, according to His glorious might, for the attaining of all steadfastness and patience; joyously giving thanks to the Father who has qualified us to share in the inheritance of the saints in Light."*
> Colossians 1:9-12

This is Paul's first prayer for the Colossians. It is a prayer that they would be filled with a knowledge of His will in all spiritual wisdom and understanding. The results of this filling, of knowing His will in this context, are that we may walk in a manner worthy of Him, please Him in all respects, bear fruit in every good work, increase in the knowledge of Him. God's part in this is strengthening us with His power for the attaining of steadfastness and patience. Our part, realizing that He has qualified us to share in the inheritance of the saints in light, is joyously giving thanks. Attaining steadfastness and patience is not your job. That is being accomplished in you by His strengthening you with His power. You don't even have to qualify for it. He has qualified you. Hallelujah! How can you not joyously give thanks? When you do, it is an expression of your faith in His working on your behalf. It not only indicates your receptivity to His work, but provides further context for being filled with a knowledge of His will. Do you want to walk worthy of Him, please Him, bear fruit, increase in the knowledge of Him? The starting place for all these things is a knowledge of His will in spiritual wisdom and understanding. And the starting place for this is His strengthening you for the attaining of steadfastness and patience, and your joyously giving thanks for what He has done to qualify you to receive your inheritance.

3. **It enables me to offer acceptable service to Him** (Hebrews 12).

Do you want your service to God to be acceptable? It isn't by working harder and harder in your strength to do whatever you think is His will. "Therefore, since we receive a kingdom which cannot be shaken, let us show gratitude, by which we may offer to God an acceptable service with reverence and awe; for our God is a consuming fire" (Heb.12:28-29). How often have you heard sermons warning that our God is a consuming fire? How often have those sermons focused on showing gratitude? As we saw in the previous chapter, Hebrews 12 demonstrates how the problems, struggles and persecutions of life serve to remind us that we need to depend on God and trust Him totally in all things, and let go of the temporal in order to know and embrace the eternal. We should do so, knowing that we receive an eternal, unshakeable kingdom, showing gratitude (because He has qualified us to inherit this kingdom). The result is that we will be able to offer to God an acceptable service. Is reverence and awe a matter of sitting quietly in church, straight-faced and dour? No, it is a matter of showing gratitude. That will sometimes be joyful and exuberant, and sometimes so amazed and in awe of God and what He's done that we stand, sit, or fall on our face in reverence. An "acceptable service" is accomplished when offered out of a heart that trusts God through all things and expresses that faith by showing gratitude. He is a consuming fire. He is working in our lives to burn every cord that binds us to what is temporal and free us to passionately, joyfully, and by faith embrace the eternal—to live a kingdom life, now and for eternity.

4. **It replaces anxiety and allows His peace to fill and guard my heart** (Philippians 4).

> *"Be anxious for nothing, but in everything by prayer and supplication with thanksgiving let your requests be made known to God, and the peace of God, which surpasses all comprehension, will guard your hearts and your minds in Christ Jesus."*
>
> Philippians 4:4-7

Here is another passage that is often preached. The part we most remember, if not that which is most emphasized when the passage is taught, is generally the last half: "the peace of God … will guard your hearts and your minds in Christ Jesus." Be at peace, and that peace will guard your heart. Know His peace, rest in Him, and everything will be okay. Don't be anxious or troubled; be at peace. But how? By prayer and supplication with thanksgiving, let your requests be made known to God. When you do, His peace will guard your hearts and your minds in Christ Jesus. If you believe that He is God, you will believe that He is capable of meeting your needs. If you believe that He is a rewarder, you will believe that He is willing to meet your needs and there is no need for anxiety. Thanksgiving replaces anxiety with an expression of faith that He is, that He is a rewarder, and that He will hear your prayers and supplications and supply all you need according to His riches in glory in Christ Jesus (Philippians 4:19).

5. **It lets His peace rule in my heart** (Colossians 3).

> *"Let the peace of Christ rule in your hearts, to which indeed you were called in one body; and be thankful. Let the word of Christ richly dwell within you, with all wisdom teaching and admonishing one another with psalms and hymns and spiritual songs, singing with thankfulness in your heart to God. Whatever you do in word or deed,*

EXTREME *Gratitude*

*do all in the name of the Lord Jesus,
giving thanks through Him to God the Father"*
Colossians 3:15-17

For me, Colossians 3:15 was always an easy one for seeing the relationship between peace and being thankful, and illustrates that relationship for the Philippians 4 passage. The part that threw me was the middle section of the verse. What did being called in one body have to do with letting His peace rule (like an umpire), and giving thanks? As a body, we as Christians, the Church, are called to the peace of Christ. That seems easy enough, but I always felt like there was more to it.

6. **It enables me to function within the body of Christ and makes my worship an example of relationship with Him to others in the body** (Colossians 3).

The next two verses, 16 and 17, also mention being thankful, but the three seemed like distinct items on a list of Christian things to do. Verse 16 talks about teaching and admonishing one another. One another, our fellow believers, the Church, is taught and reminded of the Lord by our singing psalms, hymns and spiritual songs with thanksgiving in our hearts. That is in effect what started me on this journey. As I mentioned in the Introduction, looking around in church one Sunday as we sang and there was no expression on anyone's face that reflected joy or thankfulness—passionless, bored faces routinely mouthing the old familiar words without any thought of their meaning. To that point, I thought I was going to college to prepare for the mission field. At that moment, I felt God speak to my heart that He didn't want me in foreign missions, "I have plenty for you to do in this country." At least part of that is reminding the Church that whatever you do, in word or deed, do it giving thanks through Christ to God the Father. When you sing, sing with thanksgiving. When you do, it will admonish (put in mind) and teach one another of the truth that God is real. He exists. He is worthy of praise. He is worthy of our faith. He rewards those who seek Him. We truly have reason, as a body of believers, to rejoice and give thanks.

7. **It expresses the joy that comes from faith that He is building me up in the Christian life just as it showed the joy of faith in Him to bring me into the Christian life** (Colossians 2).

> *"As you have received Christ Jesus the Lord, so walk in Him, having been firmly rooted and now being built up in Him and established in your faith, just as you were instructed, and overflowing with gratitude."*
>
> Colossians 2:6-7

The way you get in is the way you go on. You have been firmly rooted (God's doing) and are now being built up and established (God's doing). And, just as you were thankful and rejoicing and overflowing when you "got in," so should you be as you "go on." The God who saved you sanctifies you. He laid the foundation, and He's building on it. And the building up and maturing process should bring you just as much joy and thankfulness as the getting saved part did.

8. **It acknowledges God's working through all things to reconcile men to Himself and brings glory to Him** (2 Corinthians 4).

> *"For all things are for your sakes so that the grace which is spreading to more and more people may cause the giving of thanks to abound to the glory of God. Therefore we do not lose heart...."*
>
> 2 Corinthians 4:6-18

The God who said, "Let there be light," is the God who qualified us to share in the inheritance of the saints in light. Or, as Paul put it, "The God who said, 'Light shall shine out of darkness,' is the One who has shone in our hearts to give the Light of the knowledge of the glory of God in the face of Christ" (vs.6). He goes on to talk about the suffering and affliction we experience as frail humans, made of clay, and the meaning of the cross for our experiencing the crucified life and living in the power of Christ's indwelling. He echoes Hebrews 12, that the suffering in the temporal is to point us to the eternal, so that all things result in our increased faith, and in our sharing the good news. That results in more people coming to know the grace of God. That in turn results in the abounding of the giving of thanks and bringing more glory to God. So it's okay that our bodies wear out as we get older. It's okay that we get bifocals, our hair thins, our joints ache. Thank God that our inner man is being renewed daily. The decay, as he called it, of our physical body should only remind us to let go of the temporal and embrace the eternal. What's important is that our lives and our speech proclaim the grace of God—sufficient for all our needs, and the needs of a lost and dying world. That will be accomplished by, and result in, abundant, abounding thanksgiving to the glory of God.

9. **It acknowledges and honors God for proving that He is, and that He is a rewarder of those who seek Him—our supplier and provider** *(2 Corinthians 9).*

> *"For the ministry of this service is not only fully supplying the needs of the saints, but is also overflowing through many thanksgivings to God ... Thanks be to God for His indescribable gift!"*
> 2 Corinthians 9:12-15

This is another passage that is rarely preached or taught with an emphasis on thanksgiving. Verses 6-8 are often quoted when teaching about giving or tithing. "God loves a cheerful giver" (vs.7). Verse 15 is used as a jumping-off place for teaching about the incredible gift of God in giving us His Son. When you put the whole passage together it takes on a different flavor and describes a divine method of bringing glory and thanksgiving to God Himself by making His grace abound, multiplying seed, and increasing the harvest of our righteousness, so that we have an abundance for the meeting of needs, ministering to one another and showing forth the grace of God to the glory of God. This process is an indescribably wonderful gift from God. When you reflect on the passage as a whole it is awe-inspiring what God has put in place. At the core of it is that the ministry to the needs of the saints overflows through many thanksgivings to God. God is seen and recognized as the rewarder of the saints, our supplier and provider, and thanksgiving (honoring Him as God) results.

10. **It changes us from within, making God our focus, honoring Him, and keeping us from immorality in language and deed** (Ephesians 5).

> *"But immorality or any impurity or greed must not even be named among you, as is proper among saints; and there must be no filthiness and silly talk, or coarse jesting, which are not fitting, but rather giving of thanks. For this you know with certainty, that no immoral or impure person or covetous man, who is an idolater, has an inheritance in the kingdom of Christ and God."*
>
> Ephesians 5:3-5

Let that sink in. "No immoral, impure or covetous man, who is an idolater ...." This is equated to immorality, impurity, greed, and characterized by filthiness, silly talk, or coarse jesting. The alternative is giving of thanks. Just as in Romans 1, giving thanks keeps us safe from sin, and the lack of it opens the door to immorality and idolatry. So, observe your language. Is it filthy? The Greek word means deformity or ugliness, obscenity. Could deformed words be literal? Would that include taking God's name and using more "acceptable" epithets such as golly, gosh, and gee-whiz? At the very least, it certainly means offensive, ugly, unacceptable speech. In other words, there is a standard. It used to be obvious. Words that even coarse men used when alone or in each other's company, they would avoid or at the least apologize for in the company of women or Christians whom they respected. Now, even women and children unashamedly let fly with such language, not only verbally, but in public forums such as online social networks, and woe to you if you seem offended. "Silly talk" is foolish talk—moronic words—from the Greek *"morologi,"* *"Moros"* means "dull, not acute" and *"logos"* means "word." The word for jesting (*eutrapelia*) actually has a positive sense in which it refers to wittiness. The root word carries the idea of turning or changing. It's the turn of phrase that can bring a chuckle or get a point across, as when Paul, standing in chains before Agrippa, told him, "I wish to God ... not only you but also all who hear me this day, might become such as I am, except for these chains." It is also the insult that is clothed in politeness. It's the lewd or rude comment phrased in such a way as to seem innocent—descriptive of much of our culture's comedic efforts. You may not come right out and say something crude, but you say what you want in a way that suggests something crude or vulgar. Is it any less wrong to say the words than to suggest them in such a way as to put the same mental image in the listener's mind? The point here is not to make New Testament "thou shalt nots." Rather, by understanding what is unacceptable and characteristic of an evil heart, we have a basis for examining our own hearts. If these things are common parts of our vocabulary, replacing them with thankfulness to God will change us from within, making God our focus and bringing honor to Him, and at the same time, keeping us from falling into immorality, impurity and covetousness, which is idolatry.

11. **It enables us to live in peace with men and in holiness before God** (1 Thessalonians 5).

1 Thessalonians 5:18 says, "In everything give thanks; for this is God's will for you in Christ Jesus." What is? I mean,

to what does "this" refer? Giving thanks? Or to whatever part of "everything" you happen to be facing, and in which you're looking for something for which to give thanks? In other words, is God's will for you to give thanks? Or is God's will whatever is happening, and therefore you can give thanks in that situation? Or is it referring to the whole triad of verses 16-18. They all are one sentence, divided up by semicolons.

1 Thessalonians 5:12-22 contains a series of phrases that sound almost like a list of Christian commandments. It's several groups of phrases or compound sentences. The core theme seems to be in verse 13: "Live in peace with one another." Before that we are encouraged to love those who labor diligently among us. Afterward, we're encouraged to help those who are struggling and seek what is good for others. Next, we're told to rejoice, pray, and give thanks (vv.16-19). Then we're given counsel on how not to quench the Spirit.

At the heart of it is: "Rejoice evermore; pray without ceasing; in everything give thanks for this is God's will for you in Christ Jesus." I don't believe they should be separated, and I do believe "this" refers to the whole sequence. Continual rejoicing, continual prayer, and giving thanks in all situations are the will of God for us. They are also at the core of the victorious Christian life—a life of peace—here characterized by honoring those who labor for the Lord, living in peace with one another, helping the weak, seeking after good for others, not quenching the spirit or despising prophetic words, and discerning and choosing good over evil.

Verse 23 picks up with "Now may the God of peace Himself sanctify you entirely; and may your spirit and soul and body be preserved complete, without blame at the coming of our Lord Jesus Christ. Faithful is He who calls you, and He also will bring it to pass." Faithful. God is faithful. He will bring it to pass. Bring what to pass? Your sanctification, to the point of your being blameless, complete, mature at the coming of Christ. This is the Christian life simplified. Live in peace with others, honoring those who labor for the Lord, helping the weak, rejoicing, praying, giving thanks (all of which involve faith in God), and allowing His Spirit to work by not despising prophetic words, but listening with discernment to examine what you hear and hold on to what's good. All of this is realizing the God of peace Himself is the one who makes it all happen as He sanctifies you (makes you holy). Holiness isn't about the things you do. It's about Him who is holy, making you holy. The way you get in is the way you go on. He saved you, He sanctifies you. You get in by grace through faith, you go on by grace through faith. And faith both frees you to rejoice and be thankful, and is ultimately and most fully expressed by being thankful. You want peace with men and holiness before God? Be thankful.

12. **It allows us to live in peace and tranquility in a world of tribulation** (1 Timothy 2).

> *"First of all, then, I urge that entreaties and prayers, petitions and thanksgivings, be made on behalf of all men, for kings and all who are in authority, so that we may lead a tranquil and quiet life in all godliness and dignity. This is good and acceptable in the sight of God our Savior, who desires all men to be saved and to come to the knowledge of the truth."*
>
> 1 Timothy 2:1-4

Pray for all men and for kings and all who are in authority. Three different words for prayer are used here, plus thanksgiving. Why thanksgivings? We've already seen the relationship between thanksgiving and peace. Interceding for, praying for, and giving thanks to God for all men, particularly kings and all who are in authority results in leading a tranquil and quiet life in all godliness and dignity. That's definitely the result within us. Whether or not it works out that way from the perspective of those for whom we are praying may depend on them for a season. At some point, we may suffer, but we will still know God's peace. Evil can't change that. Ultimately, evil will fail, not just in eternity, but in space and time as well. As Pharaoh hardened his heart, and his heart was further hardened by God, God's people suffered—for a season. Under the Roman Empire, some emperors persecuted Christians; some left them alone. Ultimately, the Roman Empire fell. Hitler fell. Stalin fell. The Soviet Union fell. Where men are faithful to God, even under persecution, they can give thanks, and lead a tranquil and quiet life serving God. The important thing is that in all things, we trust God absolutely.

13. **It brings focus and consistency to our prayers** *(Colossians 4)*.

> *"Devote yourselves to prayer, keeping alert in it with thanksgiving."*
> Colossians 4:2

Do you ever have trouble staying focused when you pray? Does your mind wander to the day's events, or to thinking about the person for whom you are interceding, or about the nature of their need? Do you ever unintentionally pray yourself to sleep?

When you desire to devote yourself to prayer, and you find your mind getting off task, or your body wanting to doze off, give thanks. Joyfully thank the Lord for the distraction, for the person or group for whom you are praying, for the lessons of the day, for victory over the enemy, for His many blessings. Honor Him and glorify Him for who He is. Just let the thanksgiving flow out of you and keep you alert to the task at hand.

The recurring themes in all these verses have to do with peace, holiness, and bringing honor and glory to God. The ability to give thanks for all things comes from knowing God, and it enables us to know God. There is hope here. There is provision. There is faith. This is where we find and embrace our inheritance as believers. We are joint-heirs with the One who has received all things as His inheritance. This is where "all things" become ours! Good things or bad things—there is nothing to fear, nothing to run from, nothing to be anxious about—all things are in the hands of our loving Father to mold us into the image of His precious Son, and bring glory to Himself. This is where our faith comes to the level that even if He says, "Offer Isaac on the altar of sacrifice," we know that He will still fulfill His promise through Isaac even if it means raising Him from the dead.

Trusting Him (faithing Him—that He is and that He is a rewarder of those who seek Him), we can give thanks, the ultimate expression of total faith in God. Peace flows from here. Joy flows from here. There is life here. Above all, God is glorified. Let thanks flow from your heart and from your lips, *always, for all things*!

Conclusion

As indicated at the beginning, in one sense, this book is a collection of lessons learned through life experiences and the study of Scripture. For me, one of the key lessons was that these "different" lessons were not freestanding or independent of one another. Rather, they are part of a whole. Hopefully, you saw this as you read from chapter to chapter. They interconnect with one another, and they work together to give us victory in very practical application in our daily lives. To leave out part leaves a ragged hole in the tapestry God is weaving.

We begin with knowing Him. He loves you and sent His Son to break down all barriers to your having a meaningful relationship with Him. He wants you to grow in your knowledge of Him and your relationship with Him and has even taken the responsibility for your growth. He wants you to rest in the work He has done for both your salvation and your sanctification. He gives you the ability, His ability, to do His will, so that you can rest in Him. He leads you into faith and only asks that you start where you are with your little faith, and allow it to grow like a mustard seed into faith that fully grasps the faithfulness of God and His promises and purpose. His desire is that you bring glory to Him and that you become more like Christ – the very things that should be the heart's desire of every believer. He lovingly and masterfully weaves all things together to accomplish His purpose. Because He is so faithfully at work for His glory and our growth, we can trust Him to the point of being thankful for everything that He uses to accomplish His goal—and that means all things. These foundational truths keep the Christian life from becoming a religion of ritual and dead works. They bring life and power to our prayers, to our study of the Bible, to our quiet times of listening to God, to our ministry, and to our spiritual warfare.

I wanted to share the lessons of this book with our home church several years ago, and at the same time, some friends asked if I would share it with a Bible study group with whom they were meeting. To facilitate that, I prepared a study guide. The day before writing the summary to the study guide, I learned of the death of Dr. L. Jack Gray, who so heavily influence my life and thereby this work. Praise be to God that dear and precious saint now has a "completed experience." He stands now before the throne of God, with a passion even deeper than he had here on earth. That fact I'm sure is not lost on him, and most assuredly, in turn, increases the joy and the passion he is experiencing and expressing. Furthermore, he is finding expression to the love and passion he has for his savior in measures beyond what he had or could even dream of but assuredly longed for, while here on earth.

    Holy God, grant that we would have a deeper passion for you in this life. Grant that as we comprehend the full dimension of Your lavish love and grace, that we would give that love back to you with the same passion that characterized our Savior. Grant that You, Your kingdom, and Your righteousness—knowing You and loving You – would be our greatest passion and desire. As we learn to rest in You, may our experience of You find expression in worship, in praise, in thanksgiving, and in serving others to the praise of Your glory. We love you, Lord. As the blind man who first saw men walking as trees, may our love become clearer. Like the father who said, "I believe, help my unbelief," we agree, and would add, "We love, make our love grow greater and abound still more and more." And, although in this lifetime, we may not have a "completed experience," may we always give attention to hearing Your thoughts, and may we never stop growing and maturing in wisdom and knowledge and love, and in favor of both God and man.

    Holy God, You indeed are God, and You are a rewarder! Thank You, Lord. Thank You that You

EXTREME *Gratitude*

are absolutely faithful, and I can absolutely "faith" You. You have made me joint-heir with Christ to an inheritance of all things. Nothing is excluded for You are using all things to bring glory to Your name, and to mold me into the image of Your Son. And so, in my present condition, and for this situation—this "thing" that is part of "all things." I thank You.

Addendum

One Final Illustration - from Literature

Stories abound of individuals who find themselves lost and alone and fighting adversities in order to survive. There are shipwrecks, plane crashes, lost spaceships—individuals, couples, families, small groups. They all carry a common thread of pushing through against all odds and ultimately surviving. It is a popular theme that inspires us never to give up hope.

Here is a summary from my all-time favorite. Maybe you'll recognize it. This is the story of a young man who, refusing to get caught up in the humdrum of his religious upbringing, or in his family's traditional business, sought adventure at sea. He had some good fortune, made some good connections, and began to prosper. He survived a couple of frightening storms, which gave him pause to reconsider his choices, but he shrugged off any suggestion of giving up the sea.

At one point, the ship on which he sailed was captured by pirates. He lived two years as their prisoner before escaping. In time, he made it back to sea and sailed to Brazil. Here, he did leave the sea and became a planter.

As his holdings in Brazil began to prosper, some of his fellow planters came together to discuss some of their challenges. It was decided to send to Africa for supplies and slaves, and the young man was chosen to represent the group. In exchange, his supplies would be paid for by the rest.

As his ship sailed away from Brazil, it was caught in a hurricane and blown west into the Gulf of Mexico. It lodged on a reef off the shore of an island near the coast of South America. Eleven of the seventeen who had boarded the ship climbed into the ship's boat and attempted to row to shore. The storm was abating, but still strong, and the boat capsized before they made land. Our hero was the only one to make it to shore, with nothing but the clothes he wore. Over the next two weeks, he was able to make a raft and make it back to the ship. He took all the supplies he could from the ship before it finally broke apart completely in the surf and washed out to sea.

He found a small cave, made a shelter, and sorted his supplies. He had some food, grain, weapons, cable and wood, fabric, clothes, books (including 3 Bibles), paper and some ink (on which he kept a journal as long as it lasted), and other needed items. All in all, he was fairly well provisioned. In time, he discovered he was indeed on an island, and very much alone, and a good distance from any well-used trade routes.

He felt Heaven was against him, and wept inconsolably as he reflected on his situation and "why Providence should thus completely ruin its creatures and render them so absolutely miserable, so without help, abandoned, so entirely depressed, that it could hardly be rational to be thankful for such a life."

He reflected on his situation and said it was as though "Reason, as it were, put in, expostulating with me," pointing out he was better off than those who lost their lives in the shipwreck. He knew he had been able to bring a lot of supplies ashore, and his situation could have been much worse. **At this stage, though, the idea of being thankful was just irrational.**

He assessed all that he had and made a side by side list of "the comfort I enjoyed, against the miseries I suffered."

Evil	Good
I am cast upon a horrible desolate island, void of all hope of recovery.	But I am alive, and not drowned, as all my ship's company was.
I am singled out and separated, as it were, from all the world to be miserable.	But I am singled out, too, from all the ship's crew to be spared from death; and He that miraculously saved me from death can deliver me from this condition.

Evil	Good
I am divided from mankind, a solitaire, one banished from human society.	But I am not starved and perishing on a barren place, affording no sustenance.
I have no clothes to cover me.	But I am in a hot climate, where if I had clothes, I could hardly wear them.
I am without any defense or means to resist any violence of man or beast.	But I am cast on an island, where I see no wild beasts to hurt me, as I saw on the coast of Africa. And what if I had been shipwrecked there?
I have no soul to speak to, or relieve me.	But God wonderfully sent the ship in near enough to shore, that I have gotten out so many necessary things as will either supply my wants, or enable me to supply myself even as long as I live.

He was beginning to realize that even in the worst of circumstances, one could find things to be thankful for. "Upon the whole," he wrote, "here was an undoubted testimony that there was scarce any condition in the world so miserable, but there was something negative or something positive to be thankful for in it. Let this stand as a direction from the experience of the most miserable of all conditions in this world, that we may always find in it something to comfort ourselves from, and to set in the description of good and evil, on the credit side of the account."

He was not a particularly religious man when he came to the island. Several months after coming ashore, he found some plants sprouting near his cave. It turned out to be barley. At first, He thought it was a miraculous provision of God on his behalf.

Then he remembered he had brought ashore some grain sacks from the ship. Rats had gotten into the sacks and consumed the grain. Needing the sacks for something else, he had dumped the remaining husks in this spot. His "thankfulness to God's Providence began to abate."

Later he realized, "I ought to have been as thankful for so strange and unforeseen Providence as if it had been miraculous; for it was really the work of Providence as to me, that should order or appoint, that ten or twelve grains of corn should remain unspoiled (when the rats had destroyed all the rest) as if it had been dropped from Heaven; as also that I should throw it out in that particular place where, it being in the shade of a high rock, it sprang up immediately; whereas, if I had thrown it anywhere else at the time, it had been burnt up and destroyed."

Even after all this, he still gave little thought to God. As his situation became more tolerable, and he was able to make good use of the provisions he had, he thought even less about God. After being on the island several months, he took sick. As his condition worsened, and he realized there was no one to care for him, he exclaimed, "Lord! What a miserable creature am I! If I should be sick, I shall certainly die for want of help, and what will become of me!" Then he wept. The words of his father came back to him, as his father had warned him that disaster awaited him if he set out from England to go to sea. As his fever increased, he prayed what he called his first prayer: "Lord, be my help, for I am in great distress." As he began to recover, he made a point of fixing a meal to give him strength should the fever get worse. He wrote in his journal, "This was the first bit of meat I had ever asked God's blessing to, even as I could remember, in my whole life." He was finally beginning to see his need for God and that God had an interest in him.

He was beginning to understand that God cared for him and was taking care of him. His heart began to soften as he was, in essence, learning what God thought of him, and he became more thankful.

It was during this illness that he found one of the Bibles he had brought from the ship, and opened it, and began to read,

"Call on Me in the day of trouble, and I will deliver you, and thou shalt glorify Me." As he continued his recovery, those words kept coming to mind. He despaired of ever being delivered from the island, but he began to realize that God had delivered him—providing him food, clothing, shelter, and now deliverance from sickness. "And what notice had I taken of it? Had I done my part? God had delivered me, but I had not glorified Him; that is to say, I had not owned and been thankful for that as a deliverance, and how could I expect greater deliverance?" he wrote. "This touched my heart very much, and immediately I knelt down and gave God thanks aloud for my recovery from my sickness." The next day, he began in the New Testament and started seriously reading his Bible every morning and night, not worrying about how many pages or chapters. He just read, "as long as my thoughts should engage me."

The more he read, the more he became aware of the rebelliousness and sin in his life. He read, "All these things have not brought thee to repentance." He took it personally and earnestly asked God to bring him to repentance. He read in Scripture, "He is exalted a Prince and a Saviour, to give repentance, and to give remission." His response was, "I threw down the book, and with my heart as well as my hands lifted up to Heaven, in a kind of ecstasy of joy, I cried out aloud, 'Jesus, Thou Son of David, Jesus, Thou exalted Prince and Savior, give me repentance!'

"This was the first time that I could say, in the true sense of the words, that I prayed in all my life; for now I prayed with a sense of my condition, and with a true Scripture view of hope founded on the encouragement of the Word of God."

He was so horrified by his past life and sins that his life of solitude was nothing to be delivered from. He found "deliverance from sin a much greater blessing than deliverance from affliction."

Two years into his sojourn on the island, he spent the anniversary of the shipwreck in reflection. He realized he could be, and indeed was happier in his solitary life than he ever was in the company of men, living in sin and rebellion. "I gave humble and hearty thanks that God had been pleased to discover to me, even that it was possible I might be more happy in this solitary condition than I should have been in a liberty of society and in all the pleasures of the world. That He could fully make up to me the deficiencies of my solitary state and the want of human society by His presence, and the communications of His grace to my soul, supporting, comforting, and encouraging me to depend upon His Providence here, and hope for His eternal presence hereafter.... My very desires altered, my affections changed their gusts, and my delights were perfectly new, from what they were at my first coming, or indeed for the two years past."

He was making more progress and becoming more thankful. He was now reading his Bible daily. Instead of feeling the anguish of his condition, he was seeing the hand of God providing for him, and the presence of God keeping him company. He read, "I will never, never leave thee, nor forsake thee," and he believed it. No "ill consequence" mattered if God Himself had not forsaken him. He realized that he could indeed be happier right where he was than anywhere else in the world.

Here, however, he hit a snag. **He was about to thank God for bringing him to this place**, but the very thought shocked him. He couldn't bring himself to say it.

"'How canst thou be such a hypocrite,' said I, even audibly, 'to pretend to be thankful for a condition which however thou may'st endeavor to be contented with, thou wouldst rather pray heartily to be delivered from?' So I stopped there. But though I could not say I thanked God for being there, yet I sincerely gave thanks to God for opening my eyes, by whatever afflicting providences, to see the former condition of my life, and to mourn for my wickedness, and repent. I never opened the Bible or shut it, but my very soul within me blessed God for directing my friend in England, without any order of mine, to pack it up among my goods; and for assisting me afterwards to save it out of the wreck of the ship."

Three years into his sojourn, he had made a fairly decent home for himself. He was growing his crops, finding food on the island, had a decent shelter. He was growing in his relationship with God and finding joy and contentment there. He was truly thankful as he sat down to eat, "and admired the hand of God's providence, which had thus spread my table in the wilderness." He came to the insight that men often "cannot enjoy comfortably what God has given them because they see and covet something that He has not given them. All our discontents about what we want appeared to me to spring from the want of thankfulness for what we have."

When one day he found footprints along the beach of his island, he began to fear. He was afraid for his life, for his provisions, that he had not planted enough crops or raised enough goats to see him through the disaster of raiders plundering his encampment. All his negative thoughts and fears blocked out all of the hope he had been finding in his walk with the Lord. He had seen and acknowledged God's faithful provision, but now all he could see was what he feared.

After months of fretting and worrying, he awoke one morning, and the Scripture came to mind that had set him on his spiritual journey years before, "Call upon Me in the day of trouble, I will deliver, and thou shalt glorify Me." It broke over him like a wave. It comforted and cheered his heart. He prayed earnestly for deliverance and believed once again, that God would provide it. He picked up his Bible, and "the first words that presented to me were, 'Wait on the Lord, and be of good cheer, and He shall strengthen thy heart; wait, I say, on the Lord.' It is impossible to express the comfort this gave me.

In answer, I thankfully laid down the book, and was no sadder, at least not on that occasion."

When later he realized that it was not just one man who had set foot on his island, but that there was a tribe of cannibals on the nearby mainland who came to his island for ritualistic feasts on human flesh, he again found fear rising within him. Although it caused him to be more cautious, it was resolved much more quickly as he remembered to be thankful for God's provision and protection, and took comfort in how God had delivered him up to that point.

He began to see God's protection and guidance in the subtle hints and suggestions that come to mind and guide us from the path we intended to go into doing something entirely different.

On one occasion, he rescued one of the soon to be victims of the cannibals. The man stayed with him as a grateful servant and faithful friend. Eventually, he began to instruct his man about the Christian faith. Feeling inadequate to the task, he prayed and asked the Lord for help. In the process of leading the native to faith in Christ, his understanding of the Christian faith grew.

In his words: "My grief sat lighter upon me, my habitation grew comfortable to me beyond measure; and when I reflected that in this solitary life I had been confined to, I had not only been moved myself to look up to Heaven and to seek to the hand that had brought me there, but was now to be made an instrument under Providence to save the life and, for aught I knew, the soul of a poor savage, and bring him to the true knowledge of religion, and of the Christian doctrine, that he might know Christ Jesus, to know whom is life eternal; I say, when I reflected upon all these things, a secret joy ran through every part of my soul, and I frequently rejoiced that ever I was brought to this place, which I so often thought the most dreadful of all afflictions that could have befallen me. In this thankful frame, I continued all the remainder of my time."

He had begun with nothing but fear, dread, and loathing for his situation. In the end, he had reached the place where he was not just generically thankful. He was not just thankful for small things in the midst of his crisis. He was no longer just content to give thanks in his situation. He no longer felt like a hypocrite to give thanks for his situation. He was truly thankful for the very thing he had loathed. He knew God loved him and that God is faithful. He was able to give thanks **for all things**. He learned the lesson of **extreme gratitude**.

Do you recognize this story? If you have never read the book, it is likely you have seen a movie version of *Robinson Crusoe*. None of the spiritual side of the story was in the movie I saw. I'm guessing it wasn't in the version you saw, either. It is in the book, written by Daniel Defoe, in 1719.

Endnotes

Introduction
[1] Jean Ellzey, *In Him There Is No Darkness*, ©1990. Rush Printing Co, Shreveport, LA, pp. 4, 12-13.

Chapter 1
[1] Andrew Murray, *With Christ in the School of Prayer*, Fleming H. Revell/Spire Books, p. 124.
[2] Andrew Murray, *Holiest of All*, Fleming H. Revell, pp. 221-222.

Chapter 2
[1] Augustus M. Toplady, "Rock of Ages," Public Domain

Chapter 3
[1] Jessie Penn Lewis, *The Climax of the Risen Life*, (Dorset, England: Overcomer Literature Trust), p. 21.
[2] Ibid., p.22.

Chapter 4
[1] This is why the prayer promise of Mark 11:24 cannot be used to claim whatever we want. Instead, we must seek to rest in Him and to know Him, so that we may know what His thoughts are and what His works are and pray accordingly.
[2] W. M. Douglas, *Andrew Murray, and His Message*, Grand Rapids, MI: Baker Book House, 1981, p.187.
[3] Chuck Swindoll, *Grace Awakening*, Irving, TX: Word Publishing, Inc., 1990, p.109.

Chapter 5
[1] E. W. Bullinger, Critical Lexicon and Concordance to the English and Greek New Testament, Zondervan Publishing House, Grand Rapids, MI, 1973

Chapter 6

[1] Jim Hylton, *Being at Ease*, Carpenter's Son Publishing, Franklin, Tennessee, 2016, p.247.

[2] Dennis Jernigan, *Sing Over Me*, Innovo Publishing LLC, 2014, p.147.

[3] Ibid., p.147.

[4] The "smallest letter" is *yod* in Hebrew, iota in Greek. The "smallest stroke" refers to the small parts of certain letters in Hebrew, which help distinguish one letter from another. Some are so similar that just a small stroke extending from a letter is the only way to be sure what letter is intended. This small stroke was referred to by scribes or calligraphers as a "tittle." Hence, the expression "jot or tittle."

Chapter 8

[1] Jack Taylor was the first I heard say this in a Sunday sermon at AnchorChurch, Ft. Worth, TX.

[2] John Piper, *Desiring God*, Multnomah Press, Portland, OR, 1986, p. 38.

Chapter 9

[1] Piper, op.cit., pp. 24-25.

[2] Murray, op.cit., p. 165-168.

Chapter 10

[1] Piper, op.cit., pp.24-25

[2] E. W. Bullinger, op. cit., pp. 628-9.

About the Author

Raised in a Christian family, Rick believed the things he was taught and sought to live for the Lord from a young age. Believing the best way to do this was in the ministry, he pursued studies at Louisiana College and Southwestern Seminary. God's plan was a little different, apparently wanting to show that His Word applies to normal, everyday people, and not just those "in the ministry." The God Who lives in and teaches "the most eminent apostles" also lives in and teaches the "nobody."

Rick's career path is varied. While in school, he served in a variety of church and ministry positions. Since then, he's worked a variety of jobs from drug rehab counselor to Christian retail, from church janitor to sales for a major Christian record company to owning his own business to working for a big-box retailer. His role in church life through the years has been varied as well, serving as a deacon, Sunday School teacher, and home church leader.

He is a certified professional photographer, having owned his own studio for 17 years and served as president of two professional photography organizations. He is currently on the board of directors for 21st Century Santa, a Christian-owned non-profit charity that provides disaster relief and serves the needs of special needs children and their families.

Rick and his wife, Trish, have four children, eleven grandchildren, and four great-grandchildren.

Follow Rick:

website and blog:
therickcarr.com

email:
rickc@therickcarr.com

www.ingramcontent.com/pod-product-compliance
Lightning Source LLC
Chambersburg PA
CBHW070454100426
42743CB00010B/1616